# *Letters* from Toledo
## Adventures of a Female Sailor During the Cold War

Kathy Swearingen Wolf

# Contents

## Part Four: Adak, Alaska

## Part Five: Centerville Beach and Ferndale, California

# Preface

I was motivated to write this book primarily for my children, Adam Wolf and Stacy Fiscus, but for other family members as well. I enlisted in the U. S. Navy in 1977 and received many letters from family and friends during my four years in the Navy. Over time, it has become very important to me to preserve these letters. Letter writing is almost a lost art in America so I view the letters reprinted in this book as precious treasure.

The letters sent to me from relatives and friends in my hometown, Toledo, Illinois, conveyed a strong sense of family and community. The letters not only told the story of what was going on in my family from 1977-1981but ultimately helped me to tell my own story of those four years.

Some of the letters included in my memoir are actually excerpts from letters; it became obvious to me after starting this project that it would be too monotonous for the reader to read every single word of every letter. Most of the letters are printed in their entirety though.

I was raised in Toledo by my parents, Jay and Judy Wilson. I am a product of three families; the Scotts, the Swearingens, and the Wilsons. My mother was divorced from my biological father when I was very young and she remarried by the time I was four years old. I always considered my stepfather, Jay Wilson, to be my father. He's who I always called "Dad" and that is how he is referred to in this book. While I was not biologically related to the Wilsons, they were my family and they had a very positive influence on me.

This book is based on my recollections and perceptions of the events in my life during my four-year enlistment. All the events in this book are factual but the names of a few Navy people (Petty Officer Franklin, Barry, Jack, Marcus, Kory, Jacob and Robert) have been changed to protect their identity.

# Author's Note

To lessen the confusion of who's who in my family, this is a reference for the relatives whose letters I have used in this memoir:

## The Wilson Family
Judy Wilson (my mother) – married to Jay Wilson when I was in the Navy
Olive Wilson (my grandmother) – married to Harold "Red" Wilson. *Family members called him "Pap"*
H.A. Wilson (my dad's brother)
Brenda Wilson (H.A.'s wife when I was in the Navy)
Jeanie Wilson – married to Max Wilson (my dad's brother)
Alice (Wilson) Sherwood (my dad's sister)
Amy Sherwood (Alice's daughter)

## My siblings
Susan Swearingen
Eric Wilson
Troy Wilson
Scott Wilson

## The Scott Family
Nellie Scott (my great-grandmother)
Virginia Scott (my grandmother) – married to William "Bill" Scott

Joyce (Scott) Coleman (my mom's sister)
Robert "Bob" Scott (my grandfather's brother)
Mary (Scott) Matheny (my grandfather's sister)

## The Swearingen Family
Ruth Swearingen (my grandmother) – married to Theo
    Swearingen
Rita (Brandenburg) Swearingen – married to Monty
    Swearingen, my uncle, when I was in the Navy
Bob & Phyllis Swearingen (my aunt and uncle)
Roberta (Swearingen) Fritts (Bob & Phyllis's daughter)

This memoir does not contain every single letter and card I received when I was in the Navy. The above list is only representative of the letters from family included in this memoir.

*"A smooth sea never made a skilled mariner"*
– **English Proverb**

*Part One*

# Boot Camp,
# Orlando, Florida

*April-July 1977*

# Chapter 1

# Taking the plunge

I was barely 17 years old when I graduated from high school in January 1976. For me, high school ended one week and college classes began the very next week. I attended Lakeland College in Mattoon, Illinois, for one year while living at home in Toledo, Illinois but thought I was missing out on something. I heard other college friends talking about living in an apartment and I was envious. I didn't have much of a social life then and imagined that it would be much better if I lived in an apartment with other girls my age.

In January, 1977, I found a place to stay in Mattoon, Illinois; it was the upstairs of a house on Western Avenue. The family that owned the house resided downstairs. I had four roommates and I shared a bedroom with one of them. In order to pay my rent, I needed a job to support myself. So, with the help of a friend, I was hired at a lumber yard, *Construction Materials*, in Mattoon. In order to work at that job, I had to switch to night classes at Lakeland. That's when everything sort of went "south". I hated working all day and going to school at night, I hated having so little money, and I hated the thought that my life might actually stay in that sorry state for an indefinite period of time.

On a Sunday afternoon in March 1977, I was driving home to Toledo to have dinner at my parents' home. I was feeling a bit discouraged about my busy life and lack of money. I said a little prayer. The next thing I know, the U.S. Navy popped into my mind. As I drove along the Burma Road headed towards Toledo, I can recall thinking about the TV show, *McHale's Navy* (my only frame of reference for the U.S. Navy at that time). Even though it was just a TV show, there were certain things about the Navy represented in the show that appealed to me; wearing uniforms, being patriotic, belonging to a special organization, etc. The seed was planted. I continued to think about the Navy the rest of the way home. It seemed like a perfect solution to the problems I had at the time.

My mom was in the kitchen cooking when I arrived home that day. I walked into our house, sat down at my traditional spot at our snack bar in the kitchen, and asked mom what she would think of me joining the Navy. She was very positive and said she thought it would be a great opportunity to travel and meet people. Wow, that was easy! Relieved, I then went into our living room where my dad was reclined in his favorite chair, and said "Dad, what would you think of me joining the Navy?" He sat there and didn't answer right away. I remember being surprised at his silence and a little nervous. After a few seconds, he said he would talk to his brother, H.A., about it. Dad's brother had made a career of the Army so he had first-hand knowledge of working with women in the military.

Dad must have called H.A. that very day because I don't remember waiting long to get Dad's blessing (fortunately for me, H.A. gave dad a positive analysis of what his experience had been with women in the U.S. Army).

On the following Monday, I visited the Navy recruiting office in Effingham and was surprised to find one of the recruiters had a connection to Toledo. My recruiter, Jerry Ozier, had several relatives who lived in Toledo. That gave me confidence that he wouldn't steer me in the wrong direction. Jerry was very nice to me and explained that the first step would be taking the Armed

Services Vocational Aptitude Battery (ASVAB) test. This is a requirement of every person entering the Navy. It helps the recruiter to have some idea of what the recruit is capable of and of which Navy schools he/she would qualify for.

In 1977, the requirements for entry into the Navy were:

- Be 17-31 years old, but have parental consent if you are 17.
- Be a high school graduate or pass the General Educational Development (GED) Test.
- Be eligible for Navy technical schools by passing appropriate mental tests.
- Be a U.S. citizen or national.
- No marriage restrictions.

A few things stand out in my memory of that fateful day. First of all, I passed the ASVAB test with flying colors and Jerry seemed pleasantly surprised with my scores (the ASVAB test actually produced 13 different scores). He told me I scored high enough to qualify for acceptance into the Naval Academy which, truthfully, sounded good but I had little concept of what the Naval Academy was. Secondly, Jerry gave me a health questionnaire to fill out. My mom had been concerned about my allergies and diagnosis of asthma during my childhood but that ended up not being an issue. Prior to filling out the health questionnaire, Jerry instructed me to:

*"Just check all the answers 'no' to all the questions except the one asking if you have vision in both eyes. You need to check that one 'yes'."*

He also informed me I would be ineligible to join the Navy if I was allergic to bee stings. After completing the appropriate paperwork, Jerry scheduled a physical for me at the Armed Forces Examining & Entrance Station in St. Louis, Missouri on April 1st, 1977. The nicest surprise was finding out that I would be able to enter the Navy at the rank of Airman Apprentice, E-2, due to my year of college. Otherwise, I would have entered as an Airman Recruit, E-1. The difference in pay was a whopping $45.60 (before taxes) each month but I was impressed. My year in college had not been in vain.

The Navy paid for me to stay overnight in St. Louis the night before the physical. I was put up in the Warwick Motor Inn at 1428 Locust Street. Having absolutely no clue about the process of entering the service, I was tickled pink to be able to have all these freebies; a free bus ride to St. Louis, a free night in a hotel, free this, free that. It all seemed like a pretty good deal to me!

I cannot say the physical was uneventful due to one particular incident; after the physical should have been over, the doctor asked me take my hospital gown off and turn around in a circle in front of him. I had no clothing on under the hospital gown. The purpose of this, supposedly, was for him to check for any bruises on my body. So, I twirled around in my birthday in my birthday suit feeling very awkward and humiliated but not thinking I had any other options (I was 18 years old and would never have questioned a medical doctor). *Two weeks later, in boot camp, when I told my boot camp buddies this story, they were shocked. None of them had been subjected to the same "inspection" during their physicals.*

After the physical concluded, I went back home to wait out the 12 days until I needed to return to St. Louis to go into the Navy.

On April 13, 1977, I returned to St. Louis on a Greyhound bus. The strongest memory of that day was when I climbed onboard the bus in Effingham, Illinois. I had had virtually no exposure to minorities in my childhood and, therefore, it was a little bewildering to be the only white person on the bus. All the other passengers were African American. It was dark on the bus and seemed eerily silent. As I gazed out at the passengers and tried to find a seat, I saw only the whites of their eyes.

This would be one of many times in my future when I would reflect back on a song I learned at vacation bible school when I was a just a child:

> [1]*Jesus loves the little children*
> *All the children of the world*
> *Black and yellow, red and white*
> *They're all precious in His sight*
> *Jesus loves the little children of the world*

That little song gave me reassurance that there was nothing to worry about; that people all over the world are different from me and it's nothing to be scared of. I was only 18 years old and had very little life experience. Even a children's song from my small country church could be a source of great comfort.

I found a window seat on the bus and sat down next to an elderly lady. I have only a vague memory of her being very kind to me. The bus made several stops between Effingham and St. Louis and I spent most of the trip looking out my window pondering this new life of mine.

---

1    Song written by Clare H. Woolston, no copyright

After staying all night in St. Louis, I took a taxi to the airport and flew to Orlando, Florida. This was only my second time on a commercial aircraft so it was very exciting!

# Chapter 2

# Arrival in Orlando

I reported to basic training (boot camp) in Orlando, Florida, on April 14th. I was aware of only 2 or 3 other women from my hometown who had served in the military so I had a sense that I was doing something fairly unique. While I was somewhat intimidated at what lay ahead, it was also exciting to be embarking on such an adventure! While a few friends and relatives thought I was courageous for doing this, I was bored more than anything else. I've always had a thirst for adventure and a strong desire to have something special (a trip, a new friend, a new achievement) happen to me at least once a year. My life in Mattoon was not providing this adventure and I hoped the Navy would.

Arrival in Orlando was somewhat disorienting. I arrived at the base after sundown so it wasn't possible to see what the base looked like until the next morning. On that first night, all the new recruits were initially taken to a huge room to be issued uniforms and other essential materials for our time in Boot Camp. We received three different types of uniforms: dungarees (the work uniform), black and white dress uniforms, and a light blue summer uniform. We also received uniform shoes, a black rain coat, a heavy wool winter coat, a hat, a tie (for our dress uniform), and a sensible black purse/handbag (something that only old ladies would carry).

After being issued our uniforms, we were transported to the barracks. As I recall, we were allowed to choose our bed (a set of bunk beds) we wanted to sleep in. At the end of each bunk bed was a locker with two separate spaces for the girls in the connecting bunk beds. Each space had a small compartment, with a padlock, for storing our money and valuable items.

I cried myself to sleep the first night but can't remember what caused such emotion. After the excitement of sharing my big news (of joining the Navy) with all my family and friends, and of staying in hotels for free, and then flying off to Orlando, I was suddenly confronted with the reality of how much my life had been altered in a mere 24 hours. That realization, along with a heavy dose of exhaustion, was a perfect recipe for tears.

The second day in Orlando, I discovered that the grounds of the Recruit Training Facility (RTC) in Orlando, Florida were absolutely beautiful! The lawns were so well manicured and filled with palm trees, exotic plants and beautiful flowers. April was a great time of year to start boot camp in Florida; not only was the climate perfect (temperatures ranged between the 70's and 80's), but I don't remember any significant rainfall. Even though it was boot camp, it felt like a tropical paradise. The combination of sights, sounds, and smells were heavenly. Marching to and from different parts of that picturesque base was my favorite part of living there.

Our boot camp company consisted of about 58 girls and our leader's title was "Company Commander". She greeted us each and every morning and kept us on schedule for getting us to and from all the different places we needed to be during the day and evening. Company Commanders have to have at least one enlistment under their belt and be of a certain rank (although not a very high rank). Because I had no knowledge of the Navy or its rank system, I thought our Company Commander was much higher in rank and importance than she was.

One of the girls in our company was assigned to be the "Recruit Chief Petty Officer" (RCPO) and served as an assistant to the Company Commander. This position was almost always assigned to an older girl.

Recruits were expected to march in formation everywhere; we marched to and from our classes, to and from the dining facility, and to and from physical training. I loved marching and singing the cadence songs with the rest of my Company. Here's an example of one of those songs:

> [2]*Mama, Mama can't you see...*
> *What the Navy's done to me.*
> *Took away my lovin man...*
> *Now I sleep with Uncle Sam.*

> *And then all the songs would include the Sound Off lyrics:*
> *Sound off!*
> *One, two,*
> *Sound off!*
> *Three, four..*

A good percentage of our days were spent in modern, air-conditioned classrooms learning myriad aspects of the Navy and life in the military. We learned about the military rank system, the Uniform Code of Military Justice, how to use a gas mask, fire-fighting and damage control, first aid, how to fire a .45 pistol and an M-16 rifle and to disassemble and put them back together, and many other skills.

---

2   These lyrics were remembered from a Navy friend but there appears to be no known author or copyright.

Having always enjoyed school, I found the academic part of boot camp to be easy and enjoyable. Most of the physical requirements weren't that difficult either. The push-ups, sit-ups, and swimming were fairly easy for me but the one thing that nearly broke my spirit was the running qualification. That was my weak spot. I had to run 2 ¼ miles in 25 minutes which is something most healthy young women should be able to do. There were girls who weighed more than I did, and seemed much more out of shape, but I was almost always the last one or next-to-last one in our company to finish those runs. It was just torture. I had always had allergies and didn't know if it was my breathing that was the issue or just a lack of athletic ability.

Perhaps this handicap of mine had nothing to do with allergies or anything related to my breathing. When I was at my parents' home on leave one time, one of mom's dear friends was visiting. She was in my parent's dining room talking with me and my mom. I can't remember the context of the conversation but what I do vividly remember is that she declared "Kak [my nickname], yer problem is that you've got a drop-down butt like mine." Maybe that was my problem with running! I guess it makes sense; swimmers shave their bodies to make them more aerodynamic in water. Maybe it was just that simple; all that weight on my "drop-down butt" might have been playing games with gravity thereby reducing my speed. Whatever the problem was, it (the running) certainly created a lot of stress for me.

# Chapter 3

# Fifty-Seven Roommates

My boot camp "bedroom" consisted of one large room filled with enough bunk-beds and storage lockers for me and my 57 roommates. My initial impression about my roommates was that they all seemed very different. Not only were there girls from many different areas of America but also girls of different ages, different ethnic groups, and vastly different experiences in life! We had girls from small farming communities and girls from major metropolitan areas; girls fresh out of high school and girls that had already been working for several years; girls that had never had a boyfriend and girls that had already been married and divorced. The only common denominators of the 58 girls in my Company were that we were all female, we all spoke English, and we all fell within a certain weight range.

Within our company, there existed a social division; the smokers on one side, the non-smokers on the other side. Things were different at that time. Smoking was still allowed in most buildings but only in designated places. The only area in our barracks other than our gigantic "bedroom" and communal bathroom was a small lounge located at the end of the bedroom. The smokers would congregate in that lounge during mail call (and other breaks) and the non-smokers were relegated to our bunks or the floor to sit on. This always seemed terribly unfair to me.

Virtually any recruit can attest to the fact that the highlight of every boot camp day is "Mail Call." It reminded me of the times in junior high and high school when I would try out for something and then sit on "pins and needles" waiting for my name to be called when the results were released. The same thing happened with Mail Call; all the girls in our barracks room stood quietly around the Recruit Chief Petty Officer (RCPO) as we waited for her to call out our name and hand us our mail. There was nothing more thrilling than to get multiple pieces of mail but, on the other hand, it was beyond depressing if your name wasn't called out.

I savored each and every piece of mail, reading the letters over and over. I loved the anecdotes my mom would include in her letters about my brothers. All three boys, Eric, Troy, and Scott Wilson, were under the age of 13 when I enlisted and nothing brightened my day as much as hearing about their activities or receiving a letter from one of them. My mother and grandmothers were my most faithful letter writers and due to their efforts, it was seldom that I received no mail at all.

My first good friend in boot camp was a girl from southern Indiana named Marie Morgan. Marie and I came from very similar backgrounds and bonded instantly. We always sat together during mail call while reading our letters and then shared news from each other's letters. We usually sat on the floor behind our bunks so we wouldn't mess up our perfectly made beds.

The first letter I received was written by my uncle, the one my dad had called when I first broached the subjecting of enlisting in the Navy:

## Letter from H.A. Wilson
*5 Apr 77*
*Ft. Eustis, VA*

*Dear Kathy,*

*I was somewhat surprised to learn that you intended to join the service; however, I think you'll find it to be a rewarding experience.*

*About five years ago, all the services began an all-out effort to increase the number of women in the ranks. Rules were changed, working and living conditions improved, and a great deal more jobs were opened up to women. This is true in all services and I must say the drive to enlist women is working very well. I work with a couple of junior enlisted women and my assistant is a 23-year-old Second Lieutenant female. Things are changing for the better!*

*I called home over the weekend and was told that you had already enlisted in the WAVES. That sounds fine! I really don't know much about the Navy; however, I'm sure that there are many opportunities open for young women in a variety of job specialties. There are so many jobs available I couldn't start to name them.*

*The medical field is good, along with the communications-electronics area, plus computers (data processing), and personnel. I'm sure any job you select will be a good one.*

*From my experience, I'd say to remember that the first 10 or 12 weeks are the worst. After that, you'll be more familiar with what is expected of you. Sometimes training can get a little boring but remember that what you are learning will be most useful when you get to your duty station.*

*Service life is what you make it! Nothing more. It can be great and also just the opposite. Knowing you, I'd bet you'll have a ball, learn a lot about people, and generally get your head straight as to how you'll spend the rest of your life. The service is a good place to GROW!!*

*The very best of luck to you in whatever field you end up in. I'm sure you'll do very well. Work hard, stay straight, and don't be afraid to do that little extra to get the job done. There are so many mediocre people around that a good one __really__ stands out.*

*Take care and let us know how you are doing. If I can help in any way, please let me know.*

*Love, H.A., Brenda & boys*

H.A. was right; it was a pivotal time in the military for females. Being only 18 years old, I had little appreciation of just how historic the 1970's were for women in the Navy. On August 7, 1972, the Chief of Naval Operations, Admiral Elmo Zumwalt, sent a lengthy message to everyone in the Navy listing ways the Navy would work to ensure equal rights and opportunities for women in the Navy. That same year, Alene Duerk, Director of the Navy Nurse Corps became the first female appointed to the rank of Rear Admiral in the Navy. Two years later, in February 1974, Barbara Allen Rainey became the first female naval aviator in U.S. Navy history and on October 7, 1975, President Gerald Ford signed Public Law 94-106 requiring the service academies to admit women by 1976. During my enlistment, the most historic event to take place for women in the Navy occurred in October 1978; the Navy began assigning women to serve aboard selected non-combatant ships.

Women Accepted for Volunteer Emergency Service (WAVES) was the term assigned to Navy women in 1942 but when I entered into the Navy, we were referred to as Women in the Navy (WIN). We much preferred the term "WAVES" and that's what both male and female sailors usually used when referring to Navy women.

One of the interesting aspects of being a Navy woman in the 1970's was that the vast majority of people in leadership positions were males. I remember being somewhat concerned about men resenting women in the Navy but I, personally, experienced very little of that. In fact, if anything, the men seemed to enjoy having women in the workplace. The problem was not resentment as much as sexual harassment. Those were the days before sexual harassment training (which was later implemented in all military services). Occasionally, I also found the male superiors to be mildly annoyed at simply having to deal with "female issues". For the most part though, the men I worked with were usually professional and behaved themselves. Many of the older men were actually very paternal and treated the young females like daughters or nieces. In most ways, it seemed no different than any population of men and women working together.

\* \* \*

It was no surprise that one of the first letters I received was from my Grandma Virginia. She was one of the people I was closest to back home and I knew she would worry about me being away from home. Her reference to the "Democrat" refers to our hometown newspaper, the "Toledo Democrat".

### *Letter from Grandma Virginia Scott*
*April 22, 1977*

*Dear Kathy,*

*Glad to get your note. Hope all is well with you. It has been rainy here the last couple of days. Charlie and Grandad have been working in the field some. They aimed to plant some corn yesterday but it rained. I see by the Democrat that Bytha and Betty got your name in their column. I will check with your mother and if she isn't sending you the paper, I will Monday.*

*We got our TV back yesterday eve, but it didn't work any better last nite so the guy is coming over this eve to see if he can find the trouble. It doesn't turn black in the day time – just at nite. Grandad got us some new basement windows today and Vincents are to put them in for us. Ours doesn't open and then some of the glasses are broken.*

*Evelyn Oakley bought the pink house on the Burma that you used to live in.*

*Dave just called from Hawaii. I ask him if he saw McGarrett and he said no just some of his men. I sure would enjoy going there. I just told Susie I take a magazine for old people and they have a tour we might go on. She said that might be one way.*

*I really don't know any news. Take care of yourself and write when you have time. We think of you often and just want you to be happy.*

*Love, Granny*

The "McGarrett" reference is from the old TV show, "Hawaii 5-0", and "Dave" is Dave Lashmet. Grandma worked with Dave Lashmet for many years at the Country Companies Insurance office in Toledo.

\* \* \*

My mother, Judy Wilson, was my most faithful letter-writer during my time in Boot Camp. I was the first of her five children to move far from home. My sister and three brothers were still living at home when I joined the Navy. Mom kept very busy with her family and college classes but also managed to write letters to me almost every day I was in boot camp. She would often include letters from my brothers in the envelope with her letter or mail them separately. I loved reading the letters from my little brothers.

## *Letter from Mom*
*April 23, 1977*

*Dear Kathy,*

*It sounds like you are getting a good workout. The boys can hardly believe it all. It sounds like you are making it pretty good though and time will pass keeping that busy.*

*It has rained here for the last three days and the boys are really getting tired of staying inside. Kelly and Beth are up this weekend, so Troy is going to stay all night with Kelly. I think John is going to take them roller skating tonight so Troy is really excited.*

*I finished my typing class last Monday night. We took our final test and Jeanie declared the class over so I have that behind me and was ready for it to be over because there are a lot of things going on in the summer it seems.*

*Next Wednesday night will be the last night for Psychology. We have a test over the last three chapters we have studied so it won't be a very big test.*

*Betty and Bytha found out about you being in the Navy and put a paragraph in their little column. Those gals really keep up with everything that is happening.*

*Jeanie, Wilma and I went to Mattoon Friday morning and had breakfast at the Holiday Inn, then took Troy's horn back to Samuel's and I bought a few plants and flowers. But it has been so rainy ever since that I still haven't set them out.*

17

*Dad is still working weekends but thinks they may finish up in two more weeks. He is getting pretty tired of working seven days a week and says we are going to take a vacation when he finishes but I imagine then he will decide there is too much farming to be done for us to leave. His boss is from New York and has asked us to come out there and I would love to go, but I really doubt if we do.*

*Eric attempted to teach me to drive the tractor and disk last Saturday but he was a nervous wreck. He told me he was sure I was going to tear something up but I thought I made it pretty good. Since the weather has been so bad, none of us have done any farming.*

*As you can tell, I could use Typing 4 if they offered it but I really blame this old typewriter for part of it. I really bought a lemon when I got this.*

*Love, Mom*

## *Letter from Scott Wilson*  (Age 7)
*April 23, 1977*

*Dear Kathy,*

*I want a Navy shirt. I got a "Sharks" book at school. It has a lot of big words in it.*

*Mother Black had 4 kittens but 3 of them have already died. Amy is very disappointed.*

*Mom read your letter to me. It sounds like you have to get up awful early.*

*I've been getting good grades at school. And I will be glad when school is out.*

*Love,*
*Scott*

## Letter from Troy Wilson *(Age 9)*
*April 23, 1977*

*Dear Kathy,*

*How are you? I am fine. April 16, 1977, Saturday, I went to the Shrine Circus. A man was shot out of a cannon. I did not go to school last Monday, Tuesday, or Wednesday. I had a cold.*

*Would you bring me a navy shirt? I am reading a book about the navy. It is very exciting. It only has about 5 pictures. One shows the building. It's great big. Bye.*

*With love,*
*Troy*

## Letter from Eric Wilson *(age 13)*
*April 23, 1977*

*Dear Kathy,*

*How do you like the navy so far? Right now I am listening to my new KISS tape. It is a good tape. The song is Mr. Speed playing now. Last night, I babysat from 7:00 until 3:05! I made $10.00.*

*I sold my beer cans to John Ingram. I got $50.00 for them. Right now, I am pretty rich. People have been asking me if you joined the navy and if you liked it. I said you joined and as far as I know, you like it. Well, I have to go now.*

*Sincerely,*
*Eric Jay Wilson*

When I enlisted in the Navy, my grandmother, Olive Wilson, had already retired from teaching but still had a very full and active life. She liked to go to the horse races with Pap, her husband, and watch his horse, "Ben Wood" (a standard bred pacer) race and she wrote of this frequently in her letters. She also did volunteer work, was an active member of the Bradbury Free Methodist Church, and enjoyed travelling.

Grandma Olive was also a very faithful letter-writer. This was the first letter she wrote to me when I was in Boot Camp:

## *Letter from Grandma Olive Wilson*
*Sat. morn, April 23, 1977*

*Dear Kathy,*

*I got your address yesterday so thought I'd drop you a line. Weather-wise, it is a terrible day, cold, rainy, etc. I turned the oven on for a little heat, it seemed so cool in the house.*

*Phil and Alice are selling the meat market this week; the 30th will be the last day. Alice says she will be glad to be at home for awhile.*

*Dad (Pap) is trying to get his horse into another race soon maybe at Henderson, KY next week.*

*Sidney Carrell died, Rab's mother, she was 91. Her funeral is at the Cottonwood church this afternoon. I went to Mattoon shopping with Kay Everhart yesterday and we ate at Tomaso's before we came home. I got some flowers for my flower boxes. The trees & bushes are all leafed out. I dug 2-20 lb. bags of dandelions out of the yard south of the house.*

*We have to get out 1 hour earlier in the morning. Hope I make it. We are to have special music again at Sunday school.*

*It sounds like you are doing ok in your work, lots to learn, I know, but you can do it. Remember we are all proud of you and love you very much.*

*Grandma Olive & Pap & John*

### Letter from Mom
*April 27, 1977*

*Kathy,*

*We got your letter of April 20 and are <u>very</u> glad to hear that you are adjusting o.k. I know it must be very hard but anything in life worthwhile is hard.*

*Janice Kidd thinks you made a very wise decision. She says there are so many opportunities in the service and that they have upgraded it so much recently that she really would encourage anybody that was interested in it.*

*It will cost me more than $200.00 to come down for your graduation so I don't know if I will bring Eric with me. He would be charged as an adult. He really wants to go and I think it would be educational for him so I don't know what we will do.*

*I went to Arcola Sunday night and stayed with Dad. We went out for supper with some of the people he works with. They are from New York and it was quite interesting talking with them. The lady was fascinated with the Midwest and all of our open fields and big yards. They live in an apartment with two little boys and she thinks this would be a much better place to raise her children. I feel sure that it is too.*

*Love,*
*Mom*

## Letter from Mom
*Postmarked 4-29-77*

*Kathy,*

*Max and Jeannie bought Kay Walker's house and Jeanie is so excited. They are going to sell their house out at the farm.*

*Troy and Scott were thrilled with their letters from you. Scott tries to write to you but it is so hard for him that I had to end up writing for him.*

*The weather has turned kind of cool here. We had summer for two weeks and now it is almost chilly. Troy and Scott have both had sore throats but it is because they don't want to wear coats.*

*I think Eric is coming to Florida with me and he is pretty excited about it. After we found out it will cost full fare for him, he has decided to accept this as his 8$^{th}$ grade graduation present, his birthday present and anything else that comes along for the next year. So you see he has talked hard to get to come.*

*Marge is getting new carpet laid in the shoe store and has ordered a huge amount of cowboy boots. It will look like a different store before long.*

*The boys and I have planted some garden and the green beans, radishes and carrots have started coming up so it won't be long until we have to hoe it. That's when the boys will be long gone I imagine.*

*Grandma Scott called and asked for your address so I took it down and she said she would write you. She thought you would have a big time in the Navy but she was surprised that you joined. I told her we all were surprised.*

*See you in June.*
*Mom*

The reference to the shoe store in the above letter was written because my parents as well as my Uncle John Wilson and his first wife had both owned and operated the shoe store in Toledo prior to selling it to Marge Croy. It was interesting to know how the store was changing since Marge had bought it.

### *Letter from Joyce (Scott) Coleman* (my aunt)
*Monday, May 2, 1977*

*Kathy,*

*I just got to work and no one else is here yet so I decided to start you a letter. George called on the CB and said I had received a letter from you in the mail so I'll read it when I get home.*

*Your folks, Charlie and Marilyn, Dad and Mom, Grandma and Ruth, and Ruby and Harlen all came up for sandwiches and ice cream and cake last night. Charlie's and Mom's birthday is tomorrow and George's is Thursday. We had ham-salad and tuna-salad sandwiches which is much easier than grilling out. Besides, the weather has been terrible. It rained all weekend and looks like more rain today. I guess we need the rain but I hate to be out in it.*

*I don't really know much news. Everything is just the same as when you left I think. Your mom said she is planning on coming down to your graduation. That will be a nice trip for her and give you a chance to be with family again.*

*If I was there or you here, I would have a hundred questions as to what you are doing and how you are getting along but it seems hard to talk in a letter. Your letters sound pretty positive so you must be getting along better than I thought you might. People have a tendency to base things on their own experiences rather than the individual. I would probably be homesick and miserable if I were you. In the first place, I wouldn't have had the courage to sign up.*

*I have to go to Portage, Wisconsin for a week in May. It is to train me to do my job better. The agency is paying the expenses but I'm really not looking forward to it. I have never been away from George and the boys so long before.*

*I better close for now and finish this after I read your letter.*

*Joyce*

## Letter from Mom
*May 4, 1977*

*Kathy,*

*We are having a nice day here with the sun shining and a breeze.*

*Jeanie, Wilma and I went to Mattoon this morning, had breakfast at the Holiday Inn, then went to the mall for some books at Walden's. Jill had a book report due about pyramids, so Wilma wanted to get some information for her. I bought a book about hypnotism and Jeanie bought 6 or 8 books about everything. I can't believe all the books she reads. I just wish I could read as fast as she does.*

*Eric has a track meet today at Casey. He loves these district meets because he gets to leave school about noon and doesn't get back till evening. This is the second meet he has attended during the day and he loves the missing school part. I think he enjoys the meet also.*

*Troy will have to mow the yard when he gets home this evening. He won't like that I'm sure. Grandma Va. and Olive pay him so he likes to mow their yards but he hasn't talked me into paying him yet.*

*I took Grandad to Champaign yesterday to see his eye doctor. He didn't get a real good report but the doctor assured us there is nothing to be alarmed about. The fluid pressure hadn't gone down any from the last visit so the doctor had to change the drugs he is taking. It is most important that this pressure goes down or damage to the optical nerve will be done. So, we were hoping it had gone down. Now we will just have to hope it goes down by next visit.*

*We're glad to get your letters.*

*Mom*

## Letter from Grandma Virginia Scott
*May 1977*

*Dear Kathy,*

*Just took a shower – watching TV. Will write you a line. I forget if I wrote since I received the birthday card. It was very pretty and I appreciated it a lot. I got more cards than usual. Lowell gave me a real pretty card – said "to one of my favorite people" with $20 in it. Grandad gave me $20, Grandma Scott $10 and Chuck gave me $15 last week for National Secretaries Week so this afternoon, I went up to Marge's and got me 2 dresses. I like to wear dresses to church in the summer time. Your folks got me some birthstone earrings – they are small which I like very much. Joyce got me a silk rose in a bud vase with baby breath and ferns – real pretty. Troy, Scott & Eric got me two pink rosebuds. Chas. & Marilyn gave me some tea towels & dishwashing clothes. I had a real nice birthday. I talked to Roberta at Marge's. I told her about you making the drill team. I am so proud of you and I tell everyone who will listen to me. Grandad and I hated so bad to see you go. For two reasons – first, we were concerned that it might be too hard for you and then we knew we would miss you so much. After all, we have had you around for over 19 years.*

*Grandad has been driving the tractor quite a little bit for Charlie. He has his pigs and today it was too wet to farm so he & Charlie went to*

*Paris to the sale. Tomorrow nite, they are going down south of Olney to a sale.*

*Your mom took Grandad to Champaign to have his eyes checked Tues. They had a lot of trouble. They got ready to turn off the interstate at Champaign; the car died – car so hot had to get wrecker to pull it into station. They took taxi to clinic. Then taxi back. They got car cooled off, filled with water, and came home. Okay but wrecker, taxi, etc. cost about $20.*

*Kathy, don't worry about us. We are real proud of you and just want you to be happy and do good. I know you have a lot of ability and determination so I'm sure everything will turn out good for you. We think of you often and love you very much.*

*Grandma*
*Her letter included a note from my Grandad:*

---

*Hi Kathy -- We are O.K. & real proud of you – even if you lose out on drill team, don't give up. You have accomplished a lot so far – we hope the best for you & appreciate your letter.*
　　*Grandad*

---

I think I must have written home prematurely about the drill team because I'm sure I never made it onto the team. Not only do I have no memories of being on a drill team but I would never have been able to pass the running test the very first week of boot camp (which was a requirement for being on the drill team). Once I had written home about it though, I received several letters mentioning the drill team or asking me about it. I tended to be a little impulsive when writing home about good news.

### Letter from Alice (Wilson) Sherwood (my aunt)
May 5, 1977

Dear Kathy,

Sorry I haven't written to you sooner but I have been so busy closing the meat market. Now I am a housewife for the first time in 7 years and I love it.

Phil has started his softball games already. They have played 6 games and have won them all so far! Amy is loving school and has started reading. She is doing very well.

Amy and I went to Debby and Gary Darling's wedding last Saturday. It was real nice. Susie Livesay, Lori Blade, and Cindy Dunne stood up with her. I haven't and didn't see any of the gang you ran around with for awhile. Georgiana is getting married soon. Cindy Dunne is getting married in August, Susan Kirk and Jess Shoot tomorrow.

You have probably heard all of this news but I wanted to drop you a line. I will write more later when I can think of something important. Take care and keep marching. We all miss you.

Love ya,
Phil, Alice & Amy

P.S. I know you're short of time for writing so don't worry about answering this. I've read mom's cards. Be good!

(Enclosed with that letter was this sweet little note from Amy Sherwood - now Amy Robinson):

---

Dear Kathy,
I am learning to read. I like school very much. I miss you. I am learning to ride my bike.
                    Love, Amy

---

## Letter from mom:
*Postmarked May 7, 1977*

*Kathy,*

*Jerry, the Recruiter at Effingham, called to tell me he had received a letter from you. He went ahead to tell me what an honor it is to make the Drill team. It sounds like it's something to be very proud of. He said that you would perform at graduation, so I'm bringing the movie camera and the Instamatic. I think Eric can take some pictures with the instamatic while I use the movie camera.*

*I have made reservations and must write Uncle Shorty now to make some plans with him. They are leaving Florida to come to Illinois the Monday after your graduation so I hope they won't be so busy packing that weekend that I can't stay with them. It would sure make the trip expensive if we have to stay in a motel. We plan to arrive in Orlando on Wednesday evening at 6:30 pm and come back home on Sunday morning at 10:00 am. Let us know when and if we are allowed to visit you before graduation. Jerry said that after graduation, we get to visit with you but he doesn't know exactly the schedule for that day.*

*Scott has a birthday party over at Nathan's this evening and he is really excited about it. It has rained most of the day, so I'm sure Marge is excited too. They have invited the whole class.*

*Eric was home yesterday with an ear ache. I think it must be allergies from the way he described it. I made an appointment with Dr. McNeill for this evening after school.*

*I'm reading my book on hypnotism and now I'm really confused. It contradicts everything my textbook in Psychology taught us about Sigmund Freud. This is the problem with reading. An author is just a person and every person seems to have their own opinion about everything.*

*Mom*

## Letter from Naomi Sowers
*(my Sunday school teacher):*
*May 8, 1977*

*Dear Kathy,*

*Bet you will be surprised to hear from your old Sunday School teacher. Just thought you might like to know we are all thinking of you and praying for you.*

*How are you liking the Navy? We hope you are getting along real good. Everything takes time. You will meet new friends & be okay. Just hang in there.*

*Everything around here is okay. We had our Mother-Daughter banquet at the church last night. Had a real good turn-out. I think we counted 47 which is real good for us.*

*Well, school will soon be out for another year. It sure has gone fast. And getting worse all the time; two boys were expelled last week. They were caught smoking pot in the restroom. Things just keep getting worse everywhere.*

*Not too much news so will close for now, but hope this finds you okay. You will see things some of the rest of us will never see. So, Good luck and God Bless you and keep you.*

*A friend,*
*Naomi S.*

Speaking of Sunday school, we had a wonderful church in boot camp! The chapel was very colorful, very modern in design, and brightly lit with natural sunlight. The base offered a catholic service, a Jewish service, and 2 or 3 different types of protestant services. Most of us girls loved going to the "Contemporary" service because it was unlike any church service we had ever attended. The sermons were enjoyable and obviously targeted at the audience; the message was usually applicable to our trials and tribulations in boot camp. The music was also a significant factor in how upbeat the service was; it was just as enjoyable for us as listening to our favorite bands. It did not sound like church music at all! Most of us found church to be extremely therapeutic. It revived us and made us feel like we could make it through yet another week of boot camp.

### Letter from Teresa (Stitt) Owen
*May 8, 1977,*

*Dear Kathy,*

*I'm really glad to hear that you like the Navy. I had talked to Roberta last weekend and she said your mom had given Phyllis your address so I was going to call your mom and get it but when I went to the Post Office, there was your letter (so I was thinking about you).*

*The Multiple Sclerosis Club of Cumberland County has been having bake sales the past two Saturdays so I have been busy baking stuff for mom. The first bake sale was at Neoga – they made $200.00 + some dollars. But this last Saturday was the one in Toledo and they made $421.50 which was pretty darn good for a bake sale.*

*I got Georgiana's wedding invitation.*

*Friday night, I went to Susan Kirk's wedding. It was a nice wedding: candlelight services, the tuxedo's were yellow & the bridesmaids dresses were yellow. Lisa Green sang & she's pretty good. Bridesmaids were Robin Titus, Jan Rhodes and some friend I didn't know and Jo McMorris. (I can't remember which one of these girls was the maid of honor.) Groomsmen were Jess's brother, Bill Yocum, Brad Anderson & some guy I didn't know.*

*Christie Sowers & Becky were at Susan's wedding and they brought Becky's little boy. He's really a cute baby.*

*I bet when you come home in June, you will really have a good tan.*

*The Art class or club had an art sale Saturday at the Municipal Building. I didn't go in because I didn't have time.*

*Well, I hope I've enlightened you a little on what's been going on around here. Well, I better go.*

*Teresa*
*P.S. Write soon*

I grew up in a country church, the Bradbury Free Methodist Church located a few miles north of Toledo, Illinois. During my time in the military, many of my family members still attended that church and there were frequent references to it in letters from family members. While I was in boot camp, my brothers performed a Sesame Street "Grouch and Roosevelt" skit at the church and I can only imagine how entertaining they must have been.

### Letter from Mom
*Postmarked May 10, 1977:*

*Kathy,*

*The boys are still doing their Grouch and Roosevelt skit at church and everyone seems to really enjoy it.*

*Saturday, I had lunch with Angie in Newton. That is where I was when you called. She and her husband were in Robinson for the weekend. That is where his folks live. I really enjoyed seeing her. She seems to be adjusted to the change real well.*

*Eric has been having an ear ache. He went to the Doctor Friday and he said it is an infection, fungus infection I mean, which is associated with allergies. Of course!!!*

*Scott painted a little doll down at Madge's for me for Mother's Day. It really is cute, and he is pretty proud of himself. He did a very neat job but he is a pretty neat little boy.*

*Eric and I took up the carpeting in the boys' room. It was quite a job but Eric helping made it go a lot faster.*

*I got the box of clothes and didn't even open them. I will just leave them in the closet. You may need them when you are home. Keep up the good work.*

*Mom*

### Letter from Joyce (Scott) Coleman *(my aunt)*
*May 1977*

*Dear Kathy,*

*I received the good news today about you making the drill team. Mom talked as though only a few ever make it. I'm really proud of you. I'm really feeling like you made a wise decision when you joined the Navy. I was so afraid it was a mistake at the time but now I feel you are going to make the most of it. Let me know more about the drill team.*

*Greg went with the cub scouts to visit the jail this evening. He thinks he had a great time. They showed them their finger printing kit and the sheriff's car.*

*It has rained off and on for a week. It is really hot and humid here today. I suppose it has been hot for you.*

*Time is going fast for us and I hope for you. It won't be long until your graduation. I wish I could come.*

*What happened to the girls that dropped out? Did they get a discharge?*

*I suppose you have met a lot of nice people. As soon as you can write, tell me about them.*

*Love, Joyce*

The reference in the letter to the "girls that dropped out" refers to letters I had written about a couple of girls from my Company who didn't make it through boot camp. Unlike TV reality shows where you see contestants saying "Goodbye" to everyone when they're kicked off the show, there were no goodbyes in boot camp. It was a complete mystery when a girl suddenly ceased to be in our company any longer. Rumors abounded but I was never sure what to believe. I vaguely remember one girl getting discharged for psychological reasons but it was unclear whether the "psychological reasons" were minor ones (such as homesickness) or something more serious.

There were other cases of girls getting discharged because they didn't follow the rules and/or couldn't complete all the physical or academic requirements of boot camp. I'm not sure how often that happened. The easiest way to get kicked out of boot camp was simply to claim you were gay. Recruits actually did that when they were <u>not</u> gay. The policy towards gays in the military was simple; if you <u>said</u> you were gay, you were out. If you were gay but never admitted to it, it wasn't a problem. *To this day, the "Don't ask, don't tell" policy is still in effect (although maybe not for long); it prohibits the military from trying to expose gay, lesbian and bisexual service members or applicants.*

# WORK WEEK: May 13, 1977

Week Five was referred to as "work week"; recruits were given a break from the normal structure of boot camp and we were placed in work environments. It felt like we had been let out of prison. It was a wonderful reprieve from our normal schedule. I got lucky; I was put in an administrative office on base to work in a clerical position. (Many girls were given cooking or cleaning assignments at the chow hall.) This one-week respite from the normal schedule of boot camp did wonders for our morale. It gave me a good idea of what the "real" Navy would be like and I was pleasantly surprised at how normal it seemed.

---

*Note on a postcard sent __from me__ to my parents:*
*"Mom & Dad, I won't be able to write for a week. It's Work Week and we work from 4:30-8:30. A very long day as you can see! So, I'll get in touch next week sometime. Love, Kathy"*

---

The base in Orlando was a training facility for both males and females but there were strict rules regarding fraternization with the opposite sex. Comically, there were recruits in my company who thought they would absolutely die if they had to remain celibate for two months! I don't recall any of those girls getting discharged but I sure do remember the time and energy they put into discussing their plight! And I know there was hanky panky going on during Week Five; that's when we were assigned to different jobs on base and given more freedom. While we saw males on a daily basis throughout the other 7 weeks of boot camp, we were given few opportunities to communicate with them or to do <u>anything else</u> with them. For some girls, that changed during Work Week!

* * *

The letters I received in boot camp were special in a way no other letters were. For one thing, I received letters from people who normally wouldn't write to me on a regular basis but they wrote at least one letter just to show their support. This next letter is one of those. It's from my great-uncle, Bob Scott, brother of my granddad Bill Scott. I couldn't help but smile when I saw the advice at the end of this letter.

### Letter from Bob Scott (my Great-Uncle)
*May 15, 1977*

*Dear Kathy,*

*Just a note to say "hi" and let you know everyone's ok. I got your address from your great-grandma. She called your mother for it and Judy brought it down to mom's.*

*I talked to your mother last week. She told me about the drill team. She seemed real thrilled cause you liked it so well. Told me she and Eric think they're coming down for your graduation.*

*Grandma Nellie is ok. Your grandpa is getting out and helping Charlie some. His eyes are not good but maybe he's improving. As far as I know, everyone else is ok.*

*I'm real glad you like it so well and hope you can keep on the drill team.*

*Take care and remember you're not in Toledo so keep your eyes open. Love, Bob*

I kept my "eyes open" more than Uncle Bob would ever know. I had a healthy (maybe paranoid) fear of being a victim of crime. How this fear developed, I'll never know. I cannot think of anything from my childhood that was scary enough to make me think I would be hurt or victimized. My mom used to warn me and my sister about those "carnies" (carnival people) at the Toledo Fall Festival but that was about as close as I ever came to any dangerous predators.

### Letter from Mom
*Postmarked May 31, 1977*

*Dear Kathy,*

*The boys finished school this morning. They went for an hour to get their report cards. Troy stayed home though as he has burned his leg and cut his heel all in 24 hours here. I'm scared he will manage to break a leg here right before we leave. I think I will make him stay on the couch.*

*This may be the last letter from home for you as we are leaving Thursday morning to go to H.A.'s. I will take your address and drop you a card along the way. If you call home, call Grandma and I can check with her. Susan will get the mail in case you write anything about your graduation that we need to know. You can call H.A.'s if you get the chance. We will leave there on Monday probably. So, if we don't hear from you by then, we will be at the USO on Thursday night. I'm sure we can contact someone there on base if we have questions.*

*We will go to Uncle Duane's when we get to Florida. You could call them.*

*The boys got your letters today but haven't read them yet. They really enjoy getting your letters.*

*We will see you Thursday night of next week and if you get a chance to call Grandma V. or H.A.'s, that's fine.*

*Mom*

Chapter 4

# Crisis in Boot Camp

I belonged to Company 3040 under the leadership of "Petty Officer Franklin", our Company Commander. I will never forget Petty Officer Franklin. I felt an immediate clash with her. She was petite but masculine and not someone who many of the girls liked or felt a connection to. She exuded no warmth whatsoever. Despite my success in the classroom in boot camp and my ability to endure many of the more unpleasant aspects of boot camp (going into the gas chamber, running, etc.), I think Petty Officer Franklin was determined to make my life miserable from Day One.

In boot camp, recruits hear the words "attention to detail" over and over; it is the most important aspect of mental conditioning (brainwashing) during the two months of basic training. The philosophy is that if recruits do not learn how important it is to pay attention to detail, it could easily result in someone's death once we are in the "real" military and working in dangerous positions (the dramatic examples often used for this are combat situations and working on the deck of an aircraft carrier). Safety was a constant theme throughout boot camp. *As it turned out, the most dangerous thing I would do my first year in the Navy was load a stapler.*

When I went through boot camp (and I assume it's still this way), all recruits were required to stencil their names on most of their clothing items as well as other items. We had the luxury of having our uniforms cleaned for us; with so many identical uniforms, it was obvious why we needed our names stenciled on each and every piece of clothing. One day, Petty Officer Franklin decided that the stenciling on my socks was not bright enough so she "wrote up" this offense and boy, did I suffer! To this day, it's still hard to comprehend the consequence of that "offense". As I recall, that was my second or third "offense" (everyone gets at least one or two) and it resulted in me being set-back in boot camp for two weeks! I was placed in a different company, Company 3042, and I felt like my world had ended. I sobbed and sobbed and then called my mother.

I didn't mind being in Orlando an extra two weeks and I loved my new Company Commander but I was devastated at how this changed my family's plans for visiting me. Throughout the course of boot camp, my mother's plans to come to Florida for my graduation had changed; the final plan included mom, Dad, and my brothers driving to Washington D.C., then down to Fort Eustis, Virginia, to see my dad's brother and his family, and then on to Orlando for my graduation. I was set back so late in boot camp that it was too late for my parents to change the departure date for their trip. So, they went ahead with their visit to my aunt and uncle's house and drove back to Toledo. Two weeks later, my mom flew (alone) down to Orlando for my graduation.

This situation had been devastating for me but not without a few benefits. I felt such a reduction of stress being in the second company. The environment in my second company was like a bright, sunshiny day compared to the oppressive environment of being under the command of Petty Officer Franklin. In my new company, I made a wonderful friend, Anne Reese, from Canoga Park, California and had a great time getting to know her. While a transition into a second company so near the end of boot camp would be depressing for anyone, Anne made it easy for me. She was such a breath of fresh air! She was a native Californian so full of youth and optimism. It was a joy to know her and I will never forget the kindness she extended to me during those final two weeks.

After surviving the transition into Company 3042, I focused on doing everything I needed to do to get out of boot camp! My final challenge was the running test. Throughout May and June, I had struggled with the running. On the day of my test, one of my boot camp buddies ran beside me and motivated me to run faster than usual by saying "Don't you want to see Scottie? You have to pass this test so you can go home and see your little brother!" During my time in boot camp, I had talked so much about my relationship with my "baby" brother, Scottie, and she figured that was the best way to motivate me to run. She was right. I passed that wretched running test but with very few seconds to spare.

### *Letter from Grandma Virginia:*
(undated but it was at the end of boot camp)

*Dear Kathy,*

*Received your letter yesterday – glad everything is going so good for you. You mentioned you would be stationed in California. You will get to see a lot of nice things out there. There are so many things to see in the USA. It will be nice for you to be home 24 days but expect you will get bored before the time is up.*

*The boys mowed the yard and then ate dinner with us yesterday. Your mother was working at the clinic. Guess their last appointment is at 12 and then they work people out.*

*You will see in the paper where Debbie Morgan is engaged. I think Debbie is so pretty and she wears her clothes well.*

*They are doing a lot more coal mining talk. Bill Beaumont was in the other morning with a contract to buy that 160 acres of his south* *of Bradbury for $400,000. He had a check for $40,000 – 10% down payment. If Uncle Sam didn't want about ½ of it, that would be fine. Mary Greeson said they had 300 acres they were going to sell for $900,000. Maybe someday we will be rich (ha ha) and then I can fly over where ever you are and have lunch with you.*

*I sure thought you looked nice in your uniforms. I would sure like to have some pictures so I could show them off & brag. When you are home, I can get some.*

*I better get ready for church. Take care of yourself.*

*Love, Grandma*

The "24 days" Grandma mentioned in her letter referred to a program I signed up for following boot camp. The Navy has a wonderful Recruiter Assistance Program (RAP) which I was able to participate in after boot camp ended. The program allowed me to work in the Effingham Navy recruiting office for 10 days, assisting the recruiters, so I could spend extra time at home after boot camp ended. With my leave and the RAP program, I was able to spend about a month at home after boot camp which was really nice. Not only had I been very homesick in boot camp, but I had received orders to California which meant I would not have many opportunities for visiting home after moving there (due to the expense of flying home).

## *Letter from Mary (Willenborg) Kuhn*
*June 29, 1977*

*Dear Kathy,*

*I'm so glad that you're enjoying the Navy! I'm sure it's an experience of a lifetime.*

*Bill and I found another place to live (thank God)!! It's where Pappy Strole used to live on the York Road (about 1 mile east of my house). I've been so busy with the wedding & getting the house in order. But I'm having a hell of a good time doing it.*

*I really hope to see you soon & at the wedding.*

*When you get home, be sure to call soon.*

*Take care & see you later,*

*Mary*

## Letter from Grandma Olive
*July 7, 1977*

*Dear Kathy,*

*It has been so long and so much as happened since I've had a chance to write you. Our trip by bus was great. New York and Washington D.C. are great to visit and see all the wonderful man-made buildings and statues of our forefathers. The best part of the trip was getting home. I think everyone should see them once at least, then we appreciate our own home more.*

*Everyone is well except for the heat - 96 degrees yesterday and again today. The boys are cutting corn out of the beans of a morning. John is helping put in straw. Pap hoes & pulls weeds out of his peanut patch. I take Pap to ballgames and horse races. The fair is on at Marshall; we went Monday night. Newton starts this next week so we will be going there often I expect.*

*Linda Williams will be home from the hospital tomorrow but the baby can't come for 6 weeks or so. They think he will be okay. Marilyn and the kids are here this week.*

*Amy has 2 white kittens now. She is very proud of them. She calls them Samantha and Sabrina. They may have to change their names later. Ha ha*

*Mumbly plays with our cats. One of them will let her drag him around.*

*Making friends and then moving on is bad but that is service life. You will soon be home and can get caught up on everything. The Coal Company is drilling up the Burma Road on our farm now. Hope to see you soon.*

*Love, G. Olive and all*

Boot Camp ended and I was thrilled to be able to go back home and spend three weeks before going on to California. Boot camp had only been a few weeks out of the course of my life but a very meaningful few weeks. There are lessons I learned in boot camp that are still applicable to my life today.

# Part Two:

# Moffett Field, California

## *August 1977-August 1978*

Captain Quin presenting me with a Letter of Commendation

# Chapter 5

# The base and barracks life

After spending a month at home and working at the recruiting Station in Effingham, I headed to California. My first duty station was Naval Air Station, Moffett Field, California. When I arrived in California on August 6, 1977, I simply could not have imagined a base more beautiful than Moffett Field. It was like winning a "best duty station" lottery. Having never been west of Missouri, everything was new to me; the Spanish Mission architecture of the buildings on base, the layout of the base (it felt more like a small town than a military base), cute little sports cars all over the place, and good-looking sailors all over the base! Moffett Field was an aviation base so there were always sailors in flight suits everywhere. It was so different than boot camp.

Moffett Field is located about 40 miles south of San Francisco. In 1977, Moffett Field was home to several Navy maritime patrol squadrons (VP squadrons) that flew the amazing Lockheed P-3C Orion aircraft. The P-3C was a large 4-engine turboprop airplane used for maritime patrol, anti-surface warfare, anti-submarine warfare, and reconnaissance missions. A VP squadron normally consisted of about 280-300 people which included pilots, flight engineers, anti-submarine warfare operators, electricians, mechanics, and sailors in a various other jobs.

During World War II, the base was home to the USS Macon, a 785-foot dirigible blimp. At that time, the area surrounding Moffett Field area was full of fruit orchards. By the time I arrived in California, the orchards were long gone and had been replaced by companies involved in the semiconductor and computer industries. This area had become known as Silicon Valley.

In 1977, Hangar One (the hangar used for the USS Macon during WWII) was a magnificent sight to all who were lucky enough to see it up close and go inside of it. It had been built during the Depression and remains one of the largest unsupported structures in America. The floor covers 8 acres and can accommodate 10 football fields. The hangar's interior is so large that fog sometimes forms near the ceiling and occasionally condenses into "rain" inside the building.

Hangar One was so large, I took a short ride in this
hot air balloon <u>inside</u> the hangar.

\* \* \*

At Moffett Field, I was assigned to the Human Resources department in a clerical position. I was the secretary for a Navy "Career Counselor" and assistant to the Command Master Chief. The Career Counselor advised and helped sailors with decisions on their careers. This ran the gamut from advice on where to transfer to, which duty might help in advancement, how to apply to Navy schools, etc. I was pretty happy about working for the career counselor. That was primarily my job; I didn't really do much for the Command Master Chief. It was a great job for a young woman new to the Navy

Many recruits go on to an "A" school (vocational or technical school) after boot camp but I had not been scheduled for one (the price you pay for going into the Navy on such short notice). I was considered "undesignated". Because of this, even though I was assigned to a job, I would be given the opportunity to explore the different jobs in the Navy and to eventually request an "A" school. The "A" school would teach me what I needed to know in order to perform a job and then I would be stationed at a base that required my field of expertise.

I was extremely lucky to be stationed at Moffett Field and to be assigned in a clerical position with an easy work schedule. There were many less attractive places and jobs I could have been ordered to. I could have received orders to a shipyard and been put to work on the deck of a tugboat doing nothing but cleaning and painting (this always seemed to be the example given to those of us in good jobs to make us appreciate just how good we had it!). I had better-than-normal work hours, Monday through Friday, from 8-4:00 and things were pretty casual in that work environment. Sometimes, several of us would go out to lunch together and spend well over an hour at lunch but it didn't seem to matter. Later on, when I was stationed in Alaska, I would look back on those times as "the good old days".

* * *

During my first year in the Navy, I spent a significant amount of my time being homesick. It was almost like a part-time job; I went to work, worked all day, then went home to my barracks and was homesick all night. The next day, I'd get up and repeat the same schedule.

Our barracks was much like an apartment building; for each compartment, there was a central living room and three bedrooms connected to the living room. Each bedroom had its own bathroom, 3 or 4 beds (could be single twin beds or bunk beds) and three closets. Often, I'd just sit on my bunk and stare at the phone hoping it would ring (with the caller being someone from home). There were no cell phones, e-mail or internet in those days. Communication consisted of that one lonely telephone in my barracks room and hours upon hours of letter-writing. Never was there a time when the phone rang in our room that I didn't wish with all my heart that it was for me.

My homesickness was like a horrible addiction; as much as I wanted my brain to think of other things and not dwell on home, it was if there was some king of homesickness chemical being released in my brain at regular intervals. Wave after wave of homesickness would wash over me and the result would be myriad unrealistic fantasies. I can't count the number of times when I heard a loud vehicle pull into the parking lot behind my barracks and I would happily picture it being my dad! Oh, if only that could have happened even once, I would have been the happiest girl at Moffett Field. Growing up in Toledo, the sound of my dad's truck pulling into our driveway had always given me a feeling of security and contentment.

I also had the recurring fantasy of relatives deciding to surprise me by showing up at my barracks door, with no warning, to relieve me of my homesickness. Given I was 2000 miles from Toledo, this was about as unrealistic as my dad suddenly showing up in the parking lot but it didn't keep me from hoping it would happen. My homesickness was an incurable longing and I struggled with that throughout my entire enlistment.

Looking back on that time, I realize my lack of pay contributed greatly toward my plight of sitting in my barracks being homesick at Moffett Field. I made a whopping $443.10 per month, before taxes, and was given an additional $2.84 per day for food. The sum total was woefully inadequate for paying my phone bill (which was always too high), eating out too often, going to movies, and buying whatever groceries I could manage to store in my barracks room (eventually, my expenses also included a car payment and insurance). Hence, I ended up sitting in my room feeling sorry for myself way too often.

# Chapter 6

# Elvis Dies!

My first strong memory of my job at Moffett Field was sitting in my office on August 17, 1977, and getting the awful news; Elvis had died! He had been found the day before unconscious on his bathroom floor in Graceland Mansion and was later pronounced dead at 3:30 pm. I could hardly believe my bad luck. I had assumed since I was within a day's drive of Las Vegas, I might actually get to see Elvis in concert! No such luck.

Elvis Aaron Presley was only 42 years old when he died. His death seemed symbolic of my childhood being over. Growing up, I can think of no more famous celebrity than Elvis except for the Beatles. It was almost incomprehensible that he could be dead. Not only was that the talk of everyone in our building at Moffett Field but, of course, of people throughout the entire world. Even though I was the "new girl on the block" in my office, my conversation with coworkers about Elvis's death made me feel as if I had worked with those people longer than I had. It was a bonding moment for all of us; after all, everyone knew who Elvis was. It didn't matter what state you came from, what race you were, what your interests were, or what you were doing in the Navy. We all felt like we knew Elvis.

I'm quite sure I hurried back to my barracks that night so I could phone home and talk about Elvis's death to whomever answered the phone. Throughout my enlistment, any time I heard exciting news on TV or the radio, I phoned home to talk about it. If no one answered the phone at my parents' house, I'd call my Grandma Virginia. I had grown up surrounded by family. The hardest thing about my new life was not having family nearby and someone to always talk to.

Ironically, my former art teacher from Cumberland Junior and Senior High schools, Susan James, moved to Memphis, Tennessee (which is where Graceland Mansion is located) only days after Elvis's death. She sent me this letter shortly after arriving in Memphis:

## *Letter from Susan James* *(my former art teacher)*
*August 31, 1977*

*Dear Kathy,*

*We're beginning to settle in by now and have finally superceded the infantry of boxes. We were here less than a week when Elvis died and he remains in the news daily. It appears the poor man will require a body guard even in death. Truthfully, being of that era, I was an Elvis fan but I am appalled by those "middle-aged" mothers who dragged their children to the macabre and hysterical scene at Graceland Mansion so that they could see his body.*

*Anyhow, your job (and surroundings) sound great! I'm wondering where Moffett Field is located – I'm assuming closer to San Francisco as you mentioned visiting there. Now that's one city I would love to visit.*

*Sounds as if getting a date is the least of your worries now; and I'm not at all surprised. Glad to hear, though, that you're weeding out some of the offers. The hours you work, the particular job, the sunshine, etc., sound super for a young, single, and lovely person such as you... even makes me a little envious. Your independence and confidence give you the treasures and joys of life.*

*Small world you meeting someone from Manitowoc. We had a lovely house, neighbors, and neighborhood there but I wouldn't want to be back there at all! I never knew sweating could feel so good! Everyone stays in here due to the heat so I've not gotten to meet many of my neighbors (or Shannon, playmates). However, after last year in Wisconsin, this heat feels terrific to me! It's nice to rely on the constancy of the weather. I think I'm going to like it here.*

*Dick is Assistant Professor at Memphis State University and seems to like it. One thing for sure we certainly prefer his work schedule. He teaches 3 night classes but has weekends and those lovely school vacations which sounds great after last year's experiment in the oil business.*

*Hadn't heard the Cumberland news and am always glad to get it. I'll always be interested in those people after "living with them" for 10 years.*

*Keep me posted on your progress.*

> *Most sincerely,*
> *Susan*

# Chapter 7

# Weird Roomates

For my first six months in California, I didn't have a car. So I walked the two blocks to and from work every day with one of my barrack's mates, Vivien Greenwood. Vivien lived in one of the bedrooms attached to my living room but not in my room. She also worked in a small building next to the building I worked in. A few years older than me, Vivien seemed worldly and more mature than I was. She had grown up in Philadelphia and had street smarts. Culturally, we were a world apart from each other; she was an African-American woman from the big city, I was a white girl from rural Illinois. But, we clicked. I will always be grateful for her friendship. She helped fill the void of me not having family nearby and she was someone I could always count on.

Having Vivien for a friend helped lessen the disappointment of having weird roommates. I had virtually nothing in common with any of my roommates. The first roommate was a woman about 30 years old (which seemed ancient to me) named Kathleen. She was divorced and appeared to have abandoned any effort at making herself look feminine. She wore no make-up, did nothing with her hair, and dressed as if she wanted to repel men. Kathleen was smart though. I could tell from the stories she told me about her job in the Navy that she was driven and ambitious. In hindsight, I'm sure she was much more serious about her Navy job than I was because it was her career, not just a job. It also seemed clear to me that she might be the sole means of support for herself for the rest of her life. While Kathleen had her redeeming qualities, she had one habit that just drove me crazy. She sat on her twin bed night after night drinking tea out of a single crystal goblet she had purchased at the Navy Exchange. I think it made her feel a little bit special. It's a silly thing but it just drove me bonkers watching her do this and hearing the constant noise of the clinking ice in her goblet. She was a good soul though and tried to be a good roommate.

The second roommate was also an "older" girl (30-ish) from the Philippines; what I remember of her is that she was so incredibly modest that she would change into her nightgown under her bed sheets at night and then out of her nightgown in the morning in the same fashion. She was petite and had long beautiful black hair which she brushed about a zillion times every day. I hardly remember her without a hairbrush in her hand. Another frequent behavior of hers was squirting hand lotion in her hands and rubbing them over and over (reminded me of those people with OCD who wash their hands repeatedly). The benefit of that behavior was that she always smelled good. She never went anywhere, except to work, so she was a constant presence in our room every evening and most weekends. She had a Filipino boyfriend that she talked to frequently on our one and only telephone. It made me crazy seeing her on that phone for an extended period of time! What if she were preventing a call coming in for me? And if her plan was to torture me by tying up our only phone line, why couldn't she at least speak in English so I could figure out what the heck she was talking about?

My third roommate was an African-American girl. She didn't actually live in my room very long but long enough to get on my nerves. We were about the same age but didn't have much in common. She was a very pretty girl and always easy to get along with but often seemed to be off in la-la land. I remember her traipsing to and from the bathroom in a satin Japanese robe with a comb stuck in her hair. My only complaint had to do with her hair. She spent a great deal of time fixing her hair and the result was a surprising volume of little black spiral hairs left in our bathroom sink on a regular basis. Every morning when I woke up and went into the bathroom to brush my teeth, I was greeted by those little black hairs. I never quite got used to that.

At times, I wondered "how did this happen to me? How in the world did I end up with weird roommates when everyone else has such great roommates?" That was how it seemed. I watched other girls who lived together and they all appeared much more compatible with each other than I was with my roommates. It was as if my room had been designated the "weird people only" room. Looking back on that time, I have to wonder if my roommate, Kathleen, thought her younger roommates were brats, if the Filipino girl thought her American roommates smelled bad, and if the black girl thought her white roommates were terribly unstylish and boring. And what if they were all correct in their assessments?

### *Letter from Mary Kaye Carter*
*September 11, 1977*

*Dear Kathy,*

    *Wow what a lovely surprise I got when I opened my mailbox to find not 1 letter but 2 from you. I was really glad to hear from you.*
    *I had a date Saturday night with a guy from Arcola. He's a farmer, 34, (never been married), drives a big Electra 225, has a*

*very nice boat, and a big farm house. We went to the Broom Corn festival, then to the Embassy for supper. And today, we took his boat to Shelbyville and spent the day just riding around the lake. I even got to drive the boat. It was a very enjoyable day.*

*Your Jim sounds terrific. I hope I get to meet him some day. You're having such a great time. I'm so happy for you. You be careful when you go skiing and don't break anything. Just have a good time.*

*Say, I hear you have a new cousin; Charlie and Marilyn's little boy. Congrats!*

*We are having our company picnic Sunday, the 18th, and our little group will be there. Terry, Mike, Rick, Frosty and me, etc. I'm really looking forward to it. I don't know what I'm going to take; it's a potluck. They are supplying a hog and beer and pop..then we are to bring a veg and salad and/or dessert. Decisions! What'll I do?*

*Well, I'm really tired after my big day at the lake. By the way, how was L.A.? How did you like Universal Studios? Write later. Take care.*

*Love,*
*    Mk*

My first big trip exploring California was to visit a friend from boot camp, Anne Reese, in Canoga Park which was not too far from Los Angeles. Anne took me to Universal Studios and Hollywood. It felt like a dream to walk down the Hollywood Walk of Fame in front of Mann's Chinese Theater (known as Grauman's Chinese Theater prior to 1973) and see the footprints of so many famous celebrities. That was one of the first times, after enlisting in the Navy, when I was able to understand that leaving home and living far away actually had some advantages. Anne is a girl I can't forget due to her kindness towards me during the final two weeks of boot camp. She's the friend I met when I was set back in boot camp.

## *Letter from Teresa (Stitt) Owen*
*Postmarked Sept. 13, 1977*

*Dear Kathy,*

*I would have written to you sooner but your postcard didn't have your address on it. Nothing much has happened around here. We didn't go to the Fair much. I wasn't really crazy about the fair this year. We went down Monday night after the gates closed to get a pronto pup. Then, Friday night, we went down & walked around a little and left.*

*I've been getting along really great; I'm starting to wear maternity tops almost all the time. I bought a baby sleeper yesterday. It says "I love Daddy" on it. It really made Ronnie happy. Linda and I had a rummage sale last weekend. I made $86.00. That wasn't too bad. We're having it again this weekend because we still have quite a lot of stuff left. This weekend is the Fall Festival so we thought there would be a lot of people around town.*

*Well, I better go. I'll write to you after the Fall Festival.*

*Love, Teresa*

*P.S. Tell me more about your one & only! Brandi is going to be in the Little Miss Pageant.*

## *Letter from Debbie Morgan*
*September 16, 1977*

*Dear Kathy,*

*I hope you like my beautiful stationary I'm writing on. Ha! I'm here at work & wasn't busy so I thought I would write & let you know what is going on in the big towns of Toledo & Greenup.*

*As you know, this is the big Fall Festival weekend. Mark & I didn't go last night so I can't tell you anything about it. But since I have been there so many times, I'm sure it will probably be about the same as always. Mark & I went to Mattoon last night and bought a new washer & dryer (so the answer to the question in your letter - if the wedding is still on - is "yes".) We also went to the hospital to see Mark's sister, Carol, & her new baby boy. She had a pretty rough time with it. She was two weeks overdue & they took the baby cesarian. It was the biggest baby I ever saw. Brandon Reed weighed 11 pounds and 4 ounces. So you can see why she had a rough time. I guess all your other girlfriends here are doing OK. Teresa is hardly even showing yet.*

*Mom has all the dresses done & everything is under control now (I think). Susan & Jess Shoot are going to sing at the wedding. I went last night & got all the flowers lined out. The main flower is peach roses. All of them are going to be silk. They cost more but they will last so I think it will be worth it. I got my invitations last week. I sent you one, what do you think of it? (kinda different huh?) Well that's about all the excitement back here I can think of now.*

*Boy, it sounds as though I'll never see you again. You love California and most of all "Jim". So you think he is your "one and only", huh? Well, all I want for you is the best.*

*Write again and tell me about your exciting life.*
*A friend,*

*Deb*

When I first read those letters (from Mary Kaye, Teresa and Debbie), I couldn't even remember who my "one & only", Jim, was. Then, I found a picture of him in an old scrapbook and I remembered. Jim was the first sailor I dated at Moffett Field. He was a nice Catholic Italian boy but just not my type. I think we must have only had a couple of dates (so don't ask me why I ever implied he was my "one and only"). I have only one significant memory of him and it's of a story he shared with me. It involved an incident which took place in his parents' house the first time he went home on leave after joining the Navy:

*Jim had just showered and cleaned up to eat dinner. He walked down the stairway from his bedroom and went into the dining room. All of his Italian family members were already at the table including his elderly gray-haired grandmother. Jim sat down and started to help himself to the food. He quickly realized that his family members were practically frozen in place and staring at him. He realized no one else was passing the food. At first, he was confused and then it dawned on him what was happening. No one would commence eating because Jim wasn't dressed appropriately. In his family, men were expected to show up at the dinner table in nice slacks and a button-down shirt. In the few months Jim had been away from home, he had somehow forgotten this unspoken rule or possibly just thought the rule didn't apply to him anymore. After all, he was a grown man and serving his country. He learned quickly that the family rules were still in full force and he never again made the mistake of dressing down for dinner.*

This memory is a vivid one for me because the story illustrated a different culture from the one I grew up in. This was my first realization of just how different other families were from my family. The vision of the elderly Italian matriarch sitting at the table practically willing her family members not to lift a finger to eat dinner made quite an impression on me. Jim had come from a large Italian family on the east coast and I could not quite picture myself as part of that family.

That was one of the big mistakes I made in dating; I could never just relax and enjoy dating without thinking of whether or not the guy would fit into my family and whether or not I would fit into his. None of that really mattered though because there just weren't any sparks between Jim and I. That short-lived romance was doomed from the get-go.

*Chapter 8*

# My Uncle Knew What He Was Talking About

In October, 1977, I volunteered to help paint a classroom that my Division used for various classes/training. The classroom was located in another building across from the office I worked in and my barracks was only a few blocks away from both places. Since I didn't have a car, I was often bored on the weekends so I thought painting the classroom would be a great way to pass the time. I thought it sounded like fun, not work.

My superiors got all the materials for me; a ladder, paint, brushes, rollers, etc. and gave me the keys to the building. My plan was to start painting early on a Saturday morning and to be done by Sunday afternoon. As I recall, a couple of people I worked with stopped in that weekend to see how I was doing. I was perfectly content working away without any attention or fanfare and was a little surprised when they showed up.

The following Monday, after everyone had come to work, one or two of my superiors wanted to go over to the classroom to see the paint job. I was pretty pleased with my efforts but it was just a big square room; there hadn't been any major challenges in painting the room. So, I didn't feel like I deserved a huge amount of praise. Well, guess what I got? A huge amount of praise! I found this to be so funny. My only accomplishment had been to paint a single classroom over the course of a weekend. That was it. But, you would have thought I had painted 10 classrooms in half a day for all the compliments I received. It all seemed so silly.

As if the praise wasn't enough, my superiors decided I needed a formal letter of appreciation. That's the great thing about the Navy; it's one of the things that lure young people into wanting to stay in beyond their first enlistment. There is a strong emphasis on rewarding men and women who do a good job. My uncle H.A.'s words in the letter he had written me during boot camp seemed almost prophetic; *"Work hard, stay straight, and don't be afraid to do that little extra to get the job done. There are so many mediocre people around that a good one really stands out."*

He was right...at least at Moffett Field. I quickly found that not all Navy bases are created equal; while I garnered such praise over that one task at Moffett Field, I found that my superiors at my next duty stationed weren't nearly as concerned with rewarding sailors for a job well done.

### *Letter from Great-Aunt Mary (Scott) Matheny* (who lived in San Diego at the time)
*October 18, 1977*

*Dear Kathy,*

*We received your letter and are looking forward to seeing you. You didn't say what airlines but as long as we have the flight number and time, that will be no problem. We'll find that out. I was kind of excited when you called and forgot that Scott would not be here that weekend but we didn't want to change it and hopefully you can come again sometime when he is here. He would like to see you also.*

*So, we'll see you Sat., the 22$^{nd}$ at 9:30 am.*

*Bye for now.*
   *Love,*
      *Mary*

My great-aunt Mary (sister of my Grandad, Bill Scott) was one of the most beloved members of the Scott family. She spent almost all of her adult years living in San Diego with her husband, Hedge, and their son Scott (until he moved away). I knew when I moved to California that it would be a priority to visit Aunt Mary. My strongest memory of my visit to her house was the thrill of being in a <u>real home</u> (instead of the barracks) and just enjoying Aunt Mary's company.

Aunt Mary was a woman full of enthusiasm. She wanted to take me to do some touristy things in San Diego but I didn't want to impose on her and I really wanted to just relax at her house and enjoy being with a member of my family. We settled on an outing to "Old Town" which is an older section of San Diego and, afterward, she drove me around the area she lived in. We went to the local grocery store she shopped in (which seemed massive compared to the Toledo IGA) and she showed me where her church was. She also showed me a little of the neighborhood she lived in. For growing up in the country outside of Toledo, Aunt Mary had adapted quite well to living in southern California.

I felt a soulful connection to Aunt Mary. She knew what it was like to be homesick. She knew what it was like to live so far away that the best you could hope for was a trip home once a year. But she was one of the most positive people in our family. She had taken "lemons" and done a wonderful job of making "lemonade" with living so far from family. She was an inspiration to me.

## Letter from Troy  *(4 days before his 10th birthday)*
*October 20, 1977*

*Dear Kathy,*

*I'm sorry I haven't been writing to you lately.  I just can't seem to find the time.*

*I mowed the yard this evening.  I hate to mow the yard.  I can't wait till Scott learns to mow.  I have to mow our yard, Grandma Olive's yard, and Grandma Virginia's yard too.  Scott don't have to do anything.*

*Yours truly,*
*Frank*

One of the things that changed after I left Toledo is that Troy went from being called "Troy" to being called "Frank." Dad initially started calling Troy "Frank" but it quickly caught on with others in the family and around Toledo.

There were so many nicknames both within our family as well as the community of Toledo.  Over the years, when I came home on leave, it became increasingly difficult to figure out who everyone was talking about when they used nicknames!

## Letter from Scottie  *(age 7)*
*October 1977*

*Dear Kathy,*

1.  *I have been playing a lot.*
2.  *I haven't been writing you a lot.*

3.  *Grandma is having a rummage sale and I have been helping her today.*
4.  *How have you been?*
5.  *We have new cactus plants.*

*Love, Scott*

## Letter from Alice (Wilson) Sherwood *(my aunt)*
*Oct. 20, 1977*

*Dear Kathy,*

*We were so glad to hear from you again. I am so slow writing! I owe Brenda & H.A. a letter I hope to get written today and Amy owes J.J. one. She has been writing him quite a bit. She thinks she is really grown up now. She has lost two of her bottom teeth. She also has three fillings in her teeth. She is going to have bad teeth just like Phil & I. She hasn't got a chance.*

*Amy really likes school! She is learning to add & subtract. She is reading very well and she likes to so I hope she will do well in school.*

*Phil has been gone all week to Chicago to a seminar for Harvestore. His birthday was last Tuesday. He's 28 now and feels pretty old. Amy will be 6 next month. It doesn't seem like she should be that old.*

*It sounds like you're really having a good time and enjoying yourself. Now's the time to do it while you're young and single.*

*Well, I better close for now and get busy. Take care and I'll write more later.*

*Love, Alice, Phil, and Amy*

## Letter from Brenda (Whitaker) Wilson (my aunt)
Sunday, October 23, 1977

Dear Kathy,

We enjoyed hearing from you awhile back. It sounds as though you're doing fine. I'm sure the weather is beautiful there. Have you learned to surf yet? That's something I'd like to learn to do.

I sent Troy a birthday card yesterday. They sure are growing up. Bailey and H.D. both have girlfriends & it's about all I can handle. I thought it would be another 5 years before Bailey started liking girls. I guess it's all part of growing up.

I'm glad you're getting out and finding out what life has to offer before settling down.

Jay's football team ended up tied for first place so they will have to play-off the tie next weekend. He made the winning touchdown Saturday so he was thrilled. There haven't been any real injuries yet but it's getting a little rougher every time.

H.D. & Bailey start tennis lessons 2 afternoons a week next week; they are looking forward to that. H.D. is camping this weekend with scouts and Jay spent his first overnight at a friend's house last night. H.A. is away again so Bailey and I had the day to ourselves. He had a friend spend the night.

The boys are looking forward to Halloween. Jay is going to be Spiderman and H.D. & Bailey bought things like play blood, fake warts, scars, wigs, etc. to make themselves up.

I talked to Red last weekend and he said they were getting the corn out.

Take care of yourself and drop us a line when you have a chance.

Love, Brenda

# Chapter 9

# My friend, Marie (Mame)

Shortly after starting my job at Moffett Field, I got acquainted with another Navy girl who worked in the large office opposite mine. Her name was Marie-Anne Bourque; a petite redhead from a large catholic family in Plaistow, New Hampshire (a town similar to Toledo).

Marie was a Navy Personnelman. Her job consisted of maintaining personnel records of enlisted service members. She worked in an office with several other Personnelmen. She would be my partner in adventure for the remainder of my time at Moffett Field and way beyond that.

It's funny what you remember about the significant people in your life. Having known Marie for over 30 years, I have many memories of her but one of the strongest is of the car she owned when we first met. Marie's maroon Volvo 242 made a huge impression on me. That car was as foreign to me as any car could be. I grew up in the *Land of Fords and Chevys* so I found her Volvo to be more than a little odd. For one thing, the front seats were so erect that I felt like I was sitting at a dining room table. I will never forget that aspect of her car. Every time I was a passenger in it, I had the sense that I was sitting in someone's dining room. I don't think there was anything aerodynamic about the Volvo, interior or exterior. However, Marie was as proud of that car as if it were her first child! I knew better than to be too honest about my feelings of her strange automobile.

Another strong memory of Marie was her appreciation of her red hair. She was very proud of it. I had never known anyone who had red hair and <u>liked</u> having red hair so I found this quality in Marie very endearing. It kind of reminded me of the way a baby is so proud of their belly button. Marie loved talking about her red hair and, as I recall, hoped to have at least one baby with red hair. While I have never cared for red hair, Marie worked her magic on me and convinced me that <u>her</u> red hair was special.

Marie and I had not been stationed at Moffett Field for long when we met each other. One of our coworkers introduced us, thinking that we would surely have something in common being new to the Navy, single, and about the same age. I have no memory of any transition period between meeting her and feeling we were good friends. I was so happy to have a friend I felt compatible with that I regarded us as friends from that first day.

Marie is one of the most enthusiastic people I've ever met. She is dedicated to living life to the fullest and has an absolute zest for life! I always regarded myself as a bit too serious and inhibited so it was wonderful to have a friend who could always have a blast doing anything we chose to do together! My first great memory of spending time with Marie (outside of work) was when we drove down one of the main streets into Mountain View, California, in her Volvo. We came to a stop sign, Marie's eyes lit up and she looked at me and said "You want to do a Chinese Fire Drill?" I don't think I even knew what that was until she explained it. Then, we jumped out of her car, ran around the car, jumped back in the car and cracked up giggling. Believe it or not, that felt like a very daring thing for me to do! I really wasn't a person who thrived on taking risks of any kind.

There was traffic in front of us, behind us, all around us but there we were; acting like dorks. That was the first of many adventures Marie and I would have together.

We both loved to go dancing in the military clubs. It was the late 70's and disco music was all the rage. Marie and I loved meeting new people, listening to the music, and dancing the night away. The enlisted club at Moffett Field was located just a short distance behind my barracks and it was fairly inexpensive entertainment. I also felt safety was practically assured at the Moffett Field club (as well as other military clubs). Many of the young military guys we met at the club were in the same "boat" I was in - they lived in the barracks and didn't have a car so their options were fairly limited when it came to dating.

When we grew bored with the Moffett Field club, we would visit clubs on other military bases nearby. We enjoyed going to a base on Treasure Island, an island located in the San Francisco Bay between San Francisco and Oakland. We also went to the enlisted club at the Presidio, an army base in San Francisco. A military I.D. was required to gain entry into all of the military clubs so we always felt like we were among our "own". Marie and I often felt an instant camaraderie with the military guys our age.

I have no memory of going to a civilian club during those years but I know I would not have felt nearly as safe doing that. There had been some horrific crimes against women in the 70's (serial killer Ted Bundy was still on the loose at that time) and I think women were generally cautious. I know I was.

Some of the best times I had in California were the times Marie and I spent at restaurants. She and I used to go to a Mexican restaurant called "La Posada" and order strawberry daiquiris and nachos (the best nachos I've ever had in my life).

This restaurant seemed very exotic to me as I had only been in one Mexican restaurant prior to joining the Navy and it wasn't nearly as nice as La Posada.

Near the end of my year at Moffett Field, Marie and I also went to Denny's frequently. It was located just outside the main gate to the base and was a wonderful end-of-the-evening thing for us to do when we wanted one last snack before our night out ended.

At some point in that first year of our friendship, Marie realized that my family members called me "Kak". She liked the sound of that and started calling me "Kak". Of course, if she was going to call me by a nickname, I needed to do the same so she became "Mame".

## Chapter 10

# Men with power

While there is no lack of available bachelors for young women in the military (and I dated several of those), it was the men with power who made the greatest impression on me during my time at Moffett Field.

My first superior at Moffett Field was a first-class Petty Officer, a Career Counselor name "Barry". He was extremely personable and easy to talk to. Initially, we hit it off and I felt lucky to have him for a boss. Within a couple of months, though, my feelings changed. Barry was the most oversexed sailor I ever worked for. It was hard for him to get through the day without some mention of sex even though he was married. I think he fancied himself some type of sexual expert and hoped I would be his willing and naïve student. I had no intention of letting that happen! Regardless of how I responded to him though, his enthusiasm for bringing up the subject of sex never diminished. In today's Navy, I doubt that anyone could get by with his behavior because it would be considered blatant sexual harassment.

I remember sitting in my office one day, minding my own business, when Barry made his entrance. He always blew into the office like he was someone special. He had an inflated ego and an exaggerated sense of his importance in the world. Immediately upon entering the office, he plopped down a big "coffee table" book on my desk. I noticed the title was "Erotic Art" and thought "Oh geez." By the time this event took place, I had already voiced a few complaints about Barry to my Division Officer, Mr. Christenson. He was the superior who I could complain to. So, after Barry left the office, I grabbed the book, walked into Mr. Christenson's office, and griped about this latest action of Barry's. I said "Do I really have to put up with this crap?" Mr. Christenson rolled his eyes and said "Oh brother, okay, I'll talk to him."

I was young and unsure of how to handle this type of situation in the workplace. I wanted to have a good relationship with Barry but felt strongly that he needed to respect my feelings. While he may have been compelled to bring up the subject of sex every day, I didn't feel like I should have to listen to it. Even though I was only 18 years old, I was pretty sure of myself in many ways. It seemed obvious to me that Barry's primary goal was manipulation. If I had been older, perhaps I could have just been honest with him and told him to cut it out. But due to my youth and inexperience in the Navy, I had no idea just how far Barry would take this. At the time, I thought my only assurance in getting him to alter his behavior was to go up the chain of command and voice a complaint to another superior. In the end, my work relationship with Barry was certainly altered. We had gone from being able to have fun talking with each other throughout the work day to having clearly defined boundaries. From that point on, we were amicable and professional but certainly not friends.

Growing up in Toledo, I was very naïve about the actions of married men who were not faithful to their wives. I had absolutely no experience with married men being romantically interested in me. In my mind, it was simply improper and wasn't supposed to happen. Little did I know when I joined the

Navy that being married was not a deterrent for many military men interested in pursuing young female sailors.

\* \* \*

One of the men I respected most was Master Chief (NCCM) Courtland "Corky" Johnson, a one-of-kind military guy! He was one of those larger-than-life people you don't ever forget and one of the most interesting military men I've ever met. By the time our paths crossed, he had already served over 30 years in the Navy, the Army, and the Marine Corps combined. That, alone, made him unique but Master Chief Johnson also had a stature that demanded respect; he was about 6 feet tall, kept his hair very short, his uniforms immaculate, and he had a chest-full of ribbons. I had little idea what those ribbons represented but I knew he was someone to be admired and I was slightly intimidated by him.

One day, I went into his office to talk to him. After we talked, he said "Your uniform is getting a little tight, isn't it? Have you gained weight?" At that moment, I'm quite sure that all things measurable in my anatomy; blood pressure, pulse, etc. went completely haywire! I was stunned! I had yet to reprimanded, in any way, by any of my superiors except for the incident in boot camp. His comment felt like such an insult even though he had simply stated a fact. I looked up to this Master Chief with such adoration and wanted him to have a high opinion of me -- for his thoughts of me to be only positive ones. That moment could easily be defined as the low point of my year at Moffett Field. I knew one thing though. I had no choice but to figure out how to get that weight off.

Unfortunately, the food in boot camp had been wonderful! It had been rumored that a gourmet chef worked in the chow hall and I could easily believe that. I had put on weight in boot camp but was barely aware of it since I didn't have a set of scales and wore the same unattractive work clothing every day.

At Moffett Field, I didn't eat nearly as much as I had in boot camp but my choices in food weren't the healthiest. I resorted to eating fast food too often because it was convenient. I also had a sedentary job which didn't help matters. Weight restrictions apply to each and every person in the military and I was always "pushing the envelope" on the maximum weight allowed for my height. It was a constant aggravation. Military superiors are supposed to enforce the weight regulations but, in truth, it's often something that wasn't given much attention to in those days. However, that was not the case with Master Chief Johnson. He was from the old days in the Navy when things weren't nearly as lenient as they were in the 1970's. I respected him for this and admired him for his high standards; I just wished I could be an exception to his high standards for weight restrictions.

I was lucky to have a cinder track located adjacent to the side of my barracks. So, I started running (torturing myself) every day. I also initiated a hunger strike (which is what my dieting always felt like). It wasn't long before the excess weight came off but keeping that weight off was a constant struggle for the remainder of my enlistment.

While I have no clear memories of Master Chief Johnson complimenting me on my weight loss, I am sure of one thing; he never again made any negative comments regarding my appearance. If he had, I'm sure it would be seared in my memory.

\* \* \*

Another memorable military man Marie and I both adored was Lieutenant Commander Robert "Bob" Zafran. He, too, was quite unique. He was a "Mustang" (a slang term used for an officer who has formerly been enlisted). It's common for enlisted people to feel more of a bond or connection with Mustangs; not only do we assume those officers really know what it's like to be in our (enlisted) shoes but I think we also feel a certain pride in seeing one of "our own" be so successful. Enlisted people are not required to have college degrees but officers are. So, if you are enlisted and selected for an Officer Program, you are required to obtain a Bachelor's degree. Only a small percentage of enlisted people are lucky enough to be chosen for one of these programs and it's considered to be quite an accomplishment if you are. Bob Zafran was one of those lucky ones.

Before getting orders to the Naval Air Station, Mr. Zafran had worked in a VP squadron (and that's where his heart was). I think he felt like a "fish out of water" working in our building but I didn't know that until years later. He was the most energetic man I've ever worked for. In fact, it was hard for him to sit still at length. Mr. Zafran was always in a state of high energy, multi-tasking in a way I was not familiar with. Initially, this was something I found intriguing. I had never worked with anyone like this before. It was both good and bad. I felt somewhat invigorated by his energy. On the other hand, I occasionally felt like I couldn't live up to his expectations because I couldn't keep up with him!

Over time, I came to realize that Bob Zafran had a heart of gold. While I worked under him, he was a single parent with full custody of his two young daughters. His life couldn't have been easy but he was always professional and hard-working. I grew to have a tremendous amount of respect and admiration for the struggles he had overcome in life. His mother had died when he was young and he was raised by an older sister and her husband. Despite the hardships of his childhood, he had become successful in the Navy and was truly an inspiration to me (and still is to this day).

Capt. Ron Marriott (right), Commander, NAS Moffett Field, CA, presents a Moffett Field plaque to Cdr. Selectee Robert Zafran (left) upon his retirement from the U.S. Navy.

## *Letter from Grandma Olive*
*Postmarked Oct 24, 1977*

*Dear Kathy,*

*Sorry I'm so slow answering your letter. We have had lots going on and I just didn't get at writing. We had a 2-day garage sale here which took up a lot of time. Alice & Pam did most of the work. It went pretty good. The weather was beautiful.*

*Max had an accident and had to have 6 stitches below his right eye. He was very lucky. He was loading a tractor and a rod slipped and hit him in the face.*

*Troy had a party Saturday night. I'm giving him the coin collection my kids started years ago. I hope he will enjoy it.*

*I got some pretty flowers yesterday for Mother-in-Law day. Isn't that silly? More money for flower people.*

*Linda's baby weighs 9+ pounds and seem to be doing fine. She is thinking about going to work full-time soon.*

*Debbie Morgan got married Saturday.*

*I talked to Brenda yesterday. She said H.A. was in Florida. They were all well. They get out of school December 16 and plan to start home then so they will have a nice long vacation. When do you get off and for how long?*

*Dad and John McKinley are rebuilding the red shed. It was about to fall down. Jay and Susie are getting the harvesting about done. They have helped John Clark some. Jean is in the Mattoon hospital now.*

*We like our new minister and family very well. I'm glad you attend church. I know it would be very different. Maybe you can influence other young folks to attend. We had a weiner roast at Rex Evans Saturday night.*

*I hope you had a good time at Mary's. Are you going to Hawaii before Xmas?*

*Alice and I saw Mary Carter at Mattoon. She is looking forward to seeing you at Xmas.*

*Jeanie is sub-teaching quite a lot in High School. She seems to like it.*

*Well, I must get busy. It is cloudy. May rain today.*

*Love, Grandma Olive*

* * *

One of the highlights of my first year in California was my association with a friend and coworker, Anne Niemi. Anne was a civilian secretary who worked in the same office I worked in. She was in her late 20's and such a sweet person. She was a surrogate "big sister" to me and she really spoiled me. When she took vacations and went anywhere away from the bay area, she gave me the keys to both her apartment as well as her champagne-colored Datsun 280Z. I loved staying in her apartment and driving her little sports car! I couldn't believe how much she trusted me for barely knowing me. I will always remember her for her generosity.

The difference between barracks living and staying in Anne's apartment was like night and day. At Anne's, I had complete privacy, a fantastic waterbed with luxurious satin sheets, and a TV all to myself. With hindsight, what seemed like such a great life to me (Anne's life) was probably a pretty lonely life. I don't think Anne had many friends in the bay area and I doubt that she made enough money to live very well in such an expensive area of California. But, I was oblivious to most of that at the time. For me, it always felt like the ultimate gift to step into her "shoes" and live her life when she went on vacation.

## Letter from Great-Grandma Nellie Scott
*Postmarked November 2, 1977*

*8:45 am*

*It's a nice Sun Shiny morn and Ruth is raking leaves. We have been to
Dutch Pantry. We had pancakes.*
*Got your letter & it was nice to hear from you.*
*Glad you like California & it's a nice place to live I think. It was nice
you got to go to M.J.'s and Hedge's. I know they enjoyed having you.*

*We have a Bradbury Women's meeting tomorrow at Lizzie Gordon's.*
*I enjoy going up here to church for dinner.*
*I'm glad you got a good job and you see so much of the country.*
*We have been over to Dutch Pantry; I really like getting out early for
breakfast once a week.*

*2:40 pm*

*Ruth is raking leaves and we really have a lot of them.*
*Well, thanks a lot for the letter. Enjoyed it quite a bit.*

    *Bye,*
*Great Grandma*

## Chapter 11

# Party in San Francisco

I made lots of friends at Moffett Field. While most of them were on active duty in the Navy, I also made a few civilian friends. One of my friends, Cindy, was a civilian secretary who worked upstairs in the building I worked in. In addition to eating out occasionally and going to movies, we also went to an unforgettable party in San Francisco one time. Cindy thought I would really enjoy visiting her two friends at their apartment in the city. She knew that I didn't get many chances to go to someone's house or apartment off base because most of my friends lived on base in the barracks. I was excited about going to a party in San Francisco and meeting people that weren't in the military.

When we arrived at her friends' apartment, Cindy introduced me to her two friends, Sam and Chad, and then took me on a quick tour of their apartment. Cindy and I were the first guests at the party. I was relieved. I've always hated arriving last at any event. Upon meeting Sam and Chad, I thought they were both nice-looking and well dressed. They both had dark hair and dark eyes and were of medium stature. Unlike the guys in the barracks who were usually in jeans and t-shirts, these guys wore button-down shirts and nice slacks. I wasn't sure what to make of that formality and took note of it. It just seemed too formal for a small gathering in their apartment. Fortunately, I had dressed well and felt okay with what I had on. Both guys were very gracious and made Cindy and I feel at home.

The apartment was nice, but small, so it took us all of about 30 seconds for the tour. When we entered the apartment, we were immediately in the living room with a small kitchen to the right of it. There was a bedroom and bathroom at the back of the apartment. The apartment was very clean and everything was in its proper place. There were a few snacks set out on a coffee table in the small living room.

Slowly, people started arriving for the party. I was introduced to all of them; there were only 8-10 people invited. In group situations, I tend to be fairly reserved so I didn't talk much and just went into "observer" mode. I'm much more comfortable in one-on-one conversations than I am in group discussions plus I practically had "small-town girl" tattooed across my forehead; there was no way I could fake being a sophisticated San Franciscan. I thought the smartest thing to do was just sit quietly and listen to everyone else talk. The first topic of the conversation had something to do with gay politicians. I knew nothing about politics but was well aware of San Francisco's large gay population so the conversation didn't surprise me. The timing of that party would have been soon after Harvey Milk became the first openly gay man to be elected to public office in California. Looking back on that time, I'm sure he was one of the politicians discussed that evening but I was oblivious to his importance.

Moving right along, I noticed the conversation at the party slowly changed to a discussion of various Hollywood actors and actresses. Now that was something I knew more about! So my ears perked up but then I realized that the actors and actresses being discussed were all gay. Slowly, the "light bulb" lit up;

small apartment plus only one bedroom plus two men living there....okay, got it! About that time, Cindy whispered in my ear "you and I are the only straight people here" and she had this look on her face like it was all she could do to keep from bursting into giggles. She had known that we would be the only straight people there but thought it would be fun to surprise me.

For Cindy, this had been a joke. For me, it was much more than that. It was a profound realization that gay people view the world through a different "lens". From that day on, my perspective on gay people changed dramatically. I realized that they viewed themselves in much the same way minorities do. Their perception of themselves went way beyond their sexuality. It was much more like a subculture. At least, in San Francisco, it appeared to be that way.

For the rest of our evening at the "party", almost every topic of conversation had the same theme; gay people. It was really kind of boring. I was happy and relieved when Cindy decided it was time for us to split the scene. Of course, as soon as we were in the car, Cindy started laughing like the whole night had been so hilarious. I went along with her, trying to make her feel good, but my mind was elsewhere. I was trying to sort out what had just happened. Like so many people, I had preconceived notions of what gay people were like. Sam and Chad didn't fit any of the stereotypes of gay men; neither one of them appeared effeminate in any way. If I had not been told they were gay, I would never have guessed it.

As Cindy and I departed San Francisco and headed south to Moffett Field, we talked about Sam and Chad and engaged in wild speculation as to what their love life might be like. It was one of those situations in which we kind of wanted to know but kind of didn't. Just the idea of two men kissing each other on the lips was hard for me to absorb; I'm not sure I wanted my mind to wander too far beyond that. I've never forgotten that night though. It was a pivotal experience for altering my perception of the gay community.

## Chapter 12

# The Most Wonderful Flight of My Life!

*I don't have a specific date for this; I only remember that it happened during the year I was stationed at Moffett Field.*

Although I worked in an office in a nice building at Moffett Field, I occasionally was tasked with going to one of the squadrons to deliver a document or pick up something. I was fascinated by the interesting work environment for the VP sailors in the hangars. I often wished I would have been assigned to one of those hangars instead of the building I was in. For one thing, there was absolutely no shortage of good-looking aviators in those hangars! For another, I loved looking at the P-3s up close. For most of us assigned to a Naval Air base, the airplanes held a certain magic. There was just something about them that I couldn't put into words. They were majestic.

When I was in the Navy, any active duty military person could get a free ride on a military aircraft if there was space available. These flights were referred to as "hops". Since I was stationed at a Naval Air base where there were numerous squadrons and P-3 aircraft, it was pretty easy to get on one of those flights. P-3's had the capability to hold 24 people but only needed 5 people (pilots and crew) to fly the plane. Hence, there was usually room for passengers. Shortly after arriving at my base and realizing I had this extraordinary advantage, I discovered a flight going from Moffett Field to Chicago,

Illinois. Rather impulsively, I decided I would surprise my family with an impromptu visit! Looking back on it now, it seems like the plan was a little risky but I didn't care! I was homesick! The primary risk involved was that I had absolutely no guarantee of a return flight. I also had no plan of how I would get from Chicago to Toledo.

I'll never forget that flight for a variety of reasons. First, I was treated like royalty! The sailors onboard the aircraft were incredibly kind, very professional, and just wonderful. Not only were they extremely attentive to my every need but the pilot and co-pilot surprised me by letting me sit behind the controls in the cockpit. Just sitting there with that incredible view would have been great but the pilots did more than that; they also allowed me to actually <u>fly the plane</u>! I'm sure this was not exactly "legal" but I will always be grateful for that unique experience. If I remember correctly, the co-pilot remained in his seat and I was allowed to sit in the pilot's seat. Then the co-pilot showed me how to dip the airplane left and right so I understood what I needed to do in order to control the aircraft. It was the <u>THRILL of a lifetime</u>! It was beyond exhilarating. Instantly, I understood how anyone could get hooked on piloting an aircraft. It was one of those rare moments in life when I had to pinch myself to make sure I wasn't dreaming. The feeling of having that kind of power over a large aircraft was indescribable.

One of the great advantages in taking "hops" was that I could get out of my seat on the airplane and walk around and talk to other people onboard. It was nothing like being a passenger on a commercial aircraft. It was a social event! Onboard this P-3 was at least one other person, an older sailor, who was not part of the aircrew but had taken the plane to

Chicago just to get a free ride. The time I spent on the flight to Chicago allowed me to meet and talk to everyone on the airplane including that man. When I explained to him that I still had to travel a significant distance from Chicago to my hometown, Toledo, he offered to give me a ride. With hindsight, it's surprising I would have accepted a ride from a complete stranger (this would have been a 3-4 hour drive to Toledo). However, the camaraderie of military people is such that everyone feels like family and it's much easier to trust a fellow sailor than a complete stranger. Also, homesickness can bring about a feeling of desperation and a willingness to take the occasional risk.

Upon landing in Chicago, I went with this man to his car (I'm assuming that had to be a rental car but have no distinct memory of it) and we took off for Toledo! The only memory I have of that drive is just a vague recollection of the older sailor being a perfect gentleman. We arrived in Toledo in the middle of the night. I can't remember if the front door was unlocked or if I might have gone in the back door but I know I entered the house without letting anyone know I was there. I quietly crept back to my parents' bedroom, sat down on the edge of my mom's side of the bed and let her know I was home. I'm amazed she didn't have a heart attack!

# Chapter 13

# Liberation

*F*ebruary 1978

After enduring six months in California without a car, I made the decision to buy one. I had become friends with a Navy Chief Petty Officer, Gil Lopez, and he took me "under his wing" to help me buy a car. Getting the loan was easy; I was young, had a full-time job, and no debts. So, I applied at the Moffett Field Credit Union (with my dad co-signing) and, just like magic, I had the money to buy a car. I was completely clueless about financial transactions, loans, etc. and, therefore, was fascinated by how easy it was to get that first car loan! My payments were only $120 per month.

Chief Lopez strongly encouraged me to buy a Toyota; he convinced me of how dependable Toyotas were and how cheap they were to maintain. I believed him but I also felt like a bit of a traitor to my dad; not only was he a Ford man but he had also been a Ford car salesman. I just hoped he would understand and not feel like I had made a mistake.

On a sunny Saturday morning, Chief Lopez and I took off for a day of car shopping. First stop: Toyota Dealership. I found a little brown Toyota Corolla, took it for a spin, and that was that! It was the perfect little car for me. It was small, cheap, and efficient. It was dark brown but had little sparkles in the paint that made it seem rather special. I fell in love with my little brown car. It only cost $4000 brand new! The entire time I owned that car, I was constantly impressed with how well it drove/rode; many of the people I had as passengers in my car commented on the same thing. It was a fantastic little car.

Having my own car was so liberating! It was beyond wonderful to leave the base any time I wanted and get out on those magnificent California highways! There were so many wonderful places to discover in California. Despite never having much money during my Navy days, I still managed to explore many different parts of California in my new car. In fact, I visited so many cities in California, it would be impossible to list them all. I became more familiar with California than my home state of Illinois.

During the summer, one of my favorite things to do was to wake up early on weekend mornings, drive to a nearby gas station in Mountain View to buy a newspaper and some strawberry licorice, and then head to the beach in Santa Cruz. Santa Cruz was only about 40 minutes from Moffett Field. It was exactly what you would expect of a California beach town; lots of touristy shops, lots of tanned bodies in bathing suits and surfers galore. I wasn't daring enough to try surfing but enjoyed watching everyone else do it.

My plan was always the same at Santa Cruz; I searched for a place not too close to other people but also not too far from other people, laid my beach towel out, and sat down to read my newspaper. After finishing the newspaper and doing a little people-watching, I laid in the sun until it was too hot to feel like fun. I loved those mornings in Santa Cruz; I never tired of watching the ocean, of watching the children play on the beach, and of viewing the endless variety of fascinating Californians cavorting up and down the beach. Because I'm a morning person, I liked getting up early and heading to Santa Cruz but the consequence of this was being alone; it wasn't easy to find others to join me early in the morning.

*Chapter 14*

# A Pillowcase
# full of Marijuana

I took another hop my year at Moffett Field but the outcome was quite different. I can't remember where I went on this flight but it was a much shorter flight. Onboard, I became acquainted with a fellow sailor, Jack. He was very attentive to me during the flight but so was every other sailor. That's just how those flights were. I don't remember thinking Jack stood out as being different than any other sailor on the flight other than I thought he was very good-looking.

A short while before our flight ended, it came as a complete surprise when Jack asked me out to dinner. Never before had anything quite like this happened to me; meeting a tall, dark handsome stranger on an airplane and then driving off into the sunset to have dinner together! My only frame of reference for this kind of magical encounter was memories of the old *Gidget* movies (Gidget also ended up in California and went ga-ga for her man, "Moondoggie"). I marveled at the fact that these things were actually happening to ME!

After Jack's post-flight tasks were complete (the time-consuming process of finishing chores onboard the aircraft and shutting the plane down), he and I walked to the hangar's parking lot to where his little black Volkswagen was parked. Then, we took off to go have dinner together. We had a great time that night and I felt like it could easily be one of those "love-at-first-sight" situations. After eating out, he took me to his apartment and we spent most of the evening there. I returned to my barracks that night feeling like I was in the middle of a marvelous dream (or a *Gidget* movie).

We went out a few more times and I naturally assumed this was going to be my first long-term relationship with a sailor. Boy, was I wrong! A couple of weeks went by and I realized Jack seemed to have vanished. He stopped calling me and I never saw him around the base. I ran into a couple of guys from his squadron and asked them if they knew what had happened to Jack. They were nice guys and I could see that they hated to tell me the truth. Then again, I think they probably wanted me to understand how oblivious I had been. So, they spilled the beans. It was almost impossible to believe what they told me; my gorgeous guy had been caught smuggling a pillow-case full of marijuana onboard a P-3 aircraft and had been locked away in the Navy Brig (jail) at the base on Treasure Island near San Francisco. As if that wasn't enough to rock my world, my friends also informed me that Jack was married and only living alone because his wife, <u>Kathy</u>, was back in Arizona giving birth to twin babies!

I was shocked at this news and understandably devastated. It was so unsettling to realize just how deceptive this guy had been. It was times like these that I'd pull out all the old clichés that my Grandma Virginia repeated so often throughout my childhood. She taught me a lot about humanity and the world through her use of those clichés and bible verses. Swirling through my mind was "One day at a time…", "Do unto others as you would have them do unto you" and "Don't judge a person until you've walked a mile in their moccasins".

I guess I needed "closure" so I did the only thing that I could think to do. Armed with Grandma Virginia's clichés, I drove my little Toyota to Treasure Island and went to visit Jack at the Navy brig. I just had to see for myself that this nightmare was really happening to me. After parking my car in the parking lot in front of the brig, I entered the main door. The guard asked me for identification. You can imagine how I felt when he looked at my military ID card and said "Are you his wife? We have a 'Kathy' listed on his visitor list but she's his wife". I should have turned around and walked out but I was determined to confront Jack face-to-face. I said "No, I'm not his wife. I'm just a friend" and the guard let me in even though I was not an authorized visitor.

When I entered the visitors' room, there he was. His eyes lit up, he walked over to me, and gave me a big hug. Despite the warm reception, I immediately cut to the chase and asked him about "Kathy". He didn't try to deny any of it. He, of course, did what every married man does when they're cheating; he tried to justify his actions by telling me that his marriage was in trouble, blah, blah, blah. The worst thing about this confrontation was that I could still completely melt in his presence regardless of how much he lied. His big brown eyes seemed full of sadness and regret. Being a sucker for the underdog, I couldn't help but feel sorry for him but I had my pride. I was very proud of being in the Navy and the last thing I wanted was any association with characters like that. We spent a few minutes talking and then I said "Goodbye". Case closed, over and out. That was my first big lesson in how deceptive men can be.

* * *

When I was a teenager at Cumberland High School, it was pretty easy to figure out who the good guys and the bad guys were. In the 1970's, anyone with super short hair tended to be straight-laced. Most of the hippies had long hair. Long hair, in and of itself, wasn't an indicator of someone being "bad" but it occasionally gave you a glimpse into their psyche and/ or lifestyle. I became somewhat conditioned to being able to judge a person's character by their appearance and personality.

Also, in a small community, there aren't many secrets when it comes to knowing who's who, what they're like, and what their family is like. In the Navy, it was very different. We all looked alike; we all wore uniforms, we all had to adhere to regulations for hair length, body adornments (piercings), etc. All recruits enter the military with a certain amount of anonymity; no one knows anything about you and you are in complete control over what you choose to disclose to others about you and your past. It's both the blessing and the curse of being in the military. Your only knowledge of people you meet is what they reveal about themselves. The flip side of that is that it is a great opportunity to redefine yourself and how you want others to view you. You don't have to be forever defined by your successes or failures in high school.

## Chapter 15

# A few good men

Fortunately, for me, there were a few good men I went out with at Moffett Field and Mike was one of them. Upon arrival at a new base, most sailors have a check-in list of different offices they needed to visit. At Moffett Field, the list included places like the medical building (dispensary), the admin office, the disbursing office (financial matters), the Navy Exchange, and my office, the Human Resources office. For a young person in the military, it was very beneficial to identify where all the important offices were on a base after getting stationed there. Because my office was on the check-in list, I was able to meet most of the new enlisted people arriving at the Naval Air Station. That's how I met Mike.

Mike was tall, cute, charming, and had rather boyish facial features. Almost immediately after handing me his check-in list, he started flirting with me. He had that "Bill Clinton" ability to win people over by establishing eye-contact with them and making them believe they were the only important person in the room. I felt like I knew Mike within minutes of getting acquainted with him. He seemed determined that he and I would become friends if not something more serious. We both lived on base and he didn't have any friends yet so it made sense that we should get to know each other.

I met Mike near the end of my time at Moffett Field so I had adopted a mentality of realizing any romance at that point in time would be temporary. He was hard to resist though. He was funny and so "in my face" (in a cute way).

One weekend, he and I drove to Santa Cruz to go to the beach. We ended up staying on the beach until pretty late in the evening. It was dark, the stars were out, and it was very romantic or could have been very romantic. I grew up seeing images of Burt Lancaster and Deborah Kerr in the movie "From Here to Eternity" rolling around in a passionate embrace on the sandy beach while the waves nearly swallowed them up. In my mind, that would have been the ultimate beach experience with a good-looking guy but Mike and I barely knew each other. We stretched out on our beach towels and looked up at the beautiful sky but we laughed more than anything else. Mike was so funny. He was one of those guys that could find humor in almost everything. I didn't think we were very compatible with each other but I sure did enjoy the way he made me laugh.

Many of my experiences in the Navy made me think of the movies. That was my only frame of reference for some of the exciting places I ended up at or some of the unique experiences I had with friends or co-workers.

\* \* \*

One of my favorite memories is of my short relationship with a sailor, Jesse James. Yep, those really were his first and middle names, believe it or not. He was young, red-headed, and had a sweet vulnerability about him. He and I lived in barracks located next to each other. That was the one and only thing we had in common but that was enough. Jesse often surprised me with cute little notes left on the windshield of my Toyota. When you're lonely and homesick, the smallest things seem so significant. I also left notes on his car and I'm sure it made his day as much as his notes made my day. In fact, those notes were so enjoyable that I can't remember anything else about Jesse!

\* \* \*

The final boyfriend I had at Moffett Field was a sailor named "Al". Unfortunately, I also met him just a few weeks before I left California. He was attending a course in the classroom I had painted. At the time he took the course, I was assisting the instructors with that class. Al was very charming and approached me during one of the breaks to ask me a question. He said "Aren't you the girl I see running around the track behind the barracks every day?" I smiled and said "Yeah, that's me!" and he replied "Yeah, I don't think I've ever seen a girl run as slow as you do. That's why I noticed you!" and he cracked up laughing. I've always admired honesty in people. He won me over instantly.

Al was wonderful. He was successful in the Navy (had already been in a few years when I met him), he was always cheerful, and he was fun! He might have been just the one that I ended up in a permanent relationship with if not for the bad timing. By the time I met him, I had only a few weeks before transferring to another duty station.

Al gave me a little stuffed bear as a going-away gift and I named it "Albo". Al and I kept in touch for a few months after I left California but we eventually lost contact. However, Albo would stay in my life for quite some time and end up travelling thousands of miles with me.

\* \* \*

Unfortunately, I don't remember many dates in California more exciting or memorable than the beach date and the series of dates with the lying criminal. Most of the young enlisted guys didn't have that much extra money or even a car to take me out in. Also, because I came from a small town with so much familiarity, no one really felt "right" for me. In every sailor I dated, there was something so dramatically different about him from the people I grew up with that I had a hard time viewing anyone as a compatible match for me. First, I dated Jim, the Italian; then the red-headed Jesse James (but I didn't really want red-headed children) and then there was Al, who was from Puerto Rico. It was hard to decide what was good for me and what wasn't good for me; I loved the fact that these men all seemed slightly exotic but I always thought back to what my aunt Joyce had told me when I was a teenager. She told me that I shouldn't marry a man unless I thought I could live with him for a lifetime. She emphasized to me that marriage wasn't just for a year or two; it was forever.

I wasted way too much time over-analyzing every aspect of my relationships with men. I think that was a huge factor in why most of my relationships only lasted about five minutes. My aunt's advice wasn't much good for dating fun but I've always believed it was a major factor in how I chose my husband.

# Chapter 16

# Behind Closed Doors

M y time in the Navy wasn't all about boyfriends and having fun. It was also about work and school. Job specialties in the Navy are called "ratings" and there are many different ratings. I had a hard time deciding what I wanted to do. I was interested in being an Air Traffic Controller but my mother thought that would be too stressful for me (and she was probably right). I also thought about doing something that would allow me to get stationed with one of the aviation squadrons but didn't really like my options of ratings for that. It was difficult to know what suited me best. I could have taken the "easy" way out and learned a job/rating at Moffett Field by studying manuals and taking tests (versus going to an actual Navy school to learn how to do a job) and remained at Moffett Field for my entire enlistment. But I yearned to do something different. I really wanted to prove that I could do something technologically challenging.

It was the 1970's and prior to that time, many women assumed there were only two choices of vocations; nursing and education. When I was in high school, girls were encouraged to pursue any type of job they desired. We could be doctors, mechanics, pilots, accountants, etc. I had completely adopted this way of thinking and wanted very much to take advantage of this new era. And, of equal importance, I had joined the Navy to "see the world". Staying at one base in California didn't feel much like seeing the world.

So, while there were a few people urging me to take the easy way out and remain at Moffett Field, it just didn't seem logical to me. Then, as fate would have it, a Master Chief Ocean Systems Technician (OTCM) visited my building one day and my life would head in an entirely new direction because of that. He had been told I was trying to decide which "A" school to attend and he hoped to persuade me to choose his rating. In order to do this, he needed to explain what being an Ocean Systems Technician meant. However, there was a slight problem. In order to do that, he had to discuss classified information with me. To do that, I needed a secret clearance and I didn't have one. So, he broke a rule. He asked me to go into a nearby office with him, alone, and he shut the door. He then explained to me what Ocean System Technicians did even though I wasn't cleared for this information. The Master Chief made it sound far more glamorous than it actually was. Being young and impressionable, I felt this entire "James Bond" aura in that office and I was hooked. If I had had any idea what I was getting into, I probably would never have stepped foot into that office!

So, instead of staying at Moffett Field for 3 more years (which was an option), a space was reserved for me at the OT "A" school in Norfolk, Virginia, which I would transfer to in August. This was a major "fork in the road" of my life even though I didn't realize it at the time.

# Chapter 17

# Interview with a Journalist

Before leaving Moffett Field, I had one final interesting experience. During my year in California, I had become friends with the Public Affairs Officer, John Shackleton. He worked in the same building I worked in. John's office had received a request from the San Jose Mercury newspaper asking permission to interview a couple of Navy women at Moffett Field on the issue of women serving onboard ships with men. U.S. District Court Judge John Sirica had recently declared a federal law unconstitutional that prohibited Navy women from serving at sea on any vessel other than Navy transports and hospital ships. So, it wouldn't be long before large numbers of women were going to sea.

John Shackleton had to select two different military women for these interviews so he asked me if I would mind being interviewed. I couldn't think of any reason not to do it so I said "sure" and told him just to let me know when and where I needed to be for the interview. I thought it sounded kind of exciting.

When the journalist from the San Jose Mercury showed up at the base, the first decision he made was NOT to photograph me in my work environment. No, that would be too boring. Instead, we jumped in his car and headed to the opposite side of the base to the magnificent Hangar One which would make a much more interesting backdrop. This historic hangar was the focal point of Moffett Field.

Once we arrived there, the journalist posed me in front of the hangar and asked me to wave my arms up in the air as if I were gesturing while answering his questions. This was such a phony setup and I felt utterly ridiculous. We spent at least 20 minutes together and discussed the issue of women going to sea. I told the journalist that I, personally, didn't want to get stationed onboard a ship but knew many women who would probably thrive in that environment. I had been in the Navy long enough to understand that certain jobs onboard ships were not only unappealing but very tedious and mentally stifling. I, myself, would not have wanted to be assigned aboard a ship even though I certainly would have if ordered to. For the sake of the interview, I hoped to convey what I thought <u>all</u> Navy women would want to see in an article like this; that we were all individuals with individual opinions. While I was honest about how I, personally, felt about shipboard duty, I didn't want the article to be just about me. I felt comfortable with the journalist and thought he understood what I was trying to say. The interview concluded and the journalist drove me back to my office. I couldn't help but feel a little bit famous and thought it would be cool to see myself in the San Jose Mercury newspaper.

On August 7, 1978, I was aghast to see a large picture of me in the San Jose Mercury with the caption *"Kathy Swearingen... 'I don't want to go'* underneath it. It made me look like such a fool and I felt so misrepresented. There I was in front of Hangar One, waving my arms up in the air like a lunatic and appearing to scream to the heavens "I don't want to go!"

Kathy Swearingen . . . 'I don't want to go'

When I had signed the contract for my four-year enlistment, I took it seriously. I would have gone anywhere or performed any job in the Navy to the best of my ability. The picture of me with the caption underneath it made it appear that I might NOT have been so willing to fulfill the obligations of my enlistment if I had been stationed onboard a ship.

My co-workers enjoyed teasing me about the article and acted like it wasn't that big of a deal. But, to me, it felt like a big deal. I worried that I had disappointed John Shackleton and wondered if he regretted asking me to do the interview.

I learned so many valuable lessons in the military and this was one of them. Never again did I approach a newspaper article in the same naïve way I had prior to participating in this one. When I see a one-line caption in a newspaper now, I always wonder what the actual interview entailed; what the other 20 minutes of conversation included.

This was the rating badge I wore on my uniforms after graduating
from Ocean System's Technician "A" School.

*Chapter 18*

# Norfolk or bust!

My glorious and eventful year at Moffett Field ended in August 1978 when I headed to Norfolk, Virginia, in my Toyota Corolla to go to OT "A" School. And guess who went with me? My buddy, Marie! She took leave so she could join me on this incredible road trip from California to Virginia. What an adventure we had! It was just the two of us along with a couple of stuffed animals, a Rand-McNally road atlas, and an incredible sense of freedom. There was no such thing as cell phones or GPS systems in those days. We had to rely on our road atlas, highway signs, and common sense to get us from the west coast to the east coast of the United States.

Prior to our departure, Chief Lopez (the same person who had helped me buy my car), gave me all kinds of instructions on how to change a flat tire, on how important it was to take flares with me on the trip, on how dangerous it might be if I allowed my gas tank to get too low, etc. Navy Chiefs are often paternal towards young sailors and he definitely acted as my surrogate father during that time. He treated me like any loving father would treat their favorite daughter.

The great thing about leaving California on a trip heading east is that the scenery changes almost instantly! It was August, a great time of year to travel, and we were enthusiastic about the 3,000 miles that lay ahead of us. Within just a few hours of starting our trip, we had experienced several changes in landscape and lots of interesting sights.

109

We did a number of things to keep entertained on that long trip. I recall pulling off to the side of the road on either the first or second day, both of us jumping out of the car, and doing some jumping jacks. I'm pretty sure this was Marie's idea. We talked, we laughed, we commented on different sights and scenery, and we talked about guys. It was a carefree time in our lives. Planning for the future consisted of thinking only one or two months in advance (if that).

There were certain events on that long journey Marie and I will always remember. The first memorable event was driving through Salt Lake City, Utah. I'm not sure if it was my funny-looking little Toyota or my California license plate but as we drove along the highway in Salt Lake City, we were astonished at the number of people gawking at us as their cars passed us. It became increasingly funny to us as the people in car, after car, after car seemed to do the same thing! At that time of our life, we found the least little thing funny but this seemed particularly hilarious. To this day, I have no idea why we were such a spectacle on that highway!

Along on the journey with Marie and I was my stuffed animal, Albo (the one my boyfriend, Al, had given me). On our journey to Virginia, Marie and I kept Albo in the back seat. It sounds silly now but Marie and I sort of treated Albo as a third person in my car. What we did with Albo reminds me a lot of what I see people doing now days when they take photographs of an inanimate object they take on their travels. It was kind of the same thing with us (minus the photos).

\* \* \*

The most dramatic event that took place on our journey occurred in Rock Springs, Wyoming. When we arrived in Rock Springs, we had travelled over 700 miles and were more than a little bored. We pulled off the highway and into a gas station in Rock Springs and we both got out of the car. I started pumping gas and, before I knew it, I glanced over and saw Marie engaged in conversation with two cowboys. Yes, two cowboys with cowboy hats and cowboy boots. When they realized what we were doing and how far we were travelling, they encouraged us to stay overnight in Rock Springs and go dancing with them. Having always been paranoid about being a victim of crime, I wanted nothing to do with this plan. But, Marie, being much <u>less</u> paranoid, begged me to stay in Rock Springs and go dancing with these cowboys. As I said earlier, Marie has an incredible enthusiasm for life and can be very hard to resist when she's bubbling over with excitement about doing something new. I certainly was tired of driving but thought Marie had possibly lost her mind. What was she thinking?

I eventually succumbed to this plan of dancing with cowboys even though every cell in my body was screaming "DON'T DO IT!" I parked my car somewhere (can't remember where) and we loaded up into one of the cowboy's pick-up trucks. Marie and I were sandwiched between the two guys in the front seat of the truck. Within minutes of getting situated, one of the cowboys said he would like to show us "White Mountain" before going dancing. The other cowboy also tried to convince us of what a good idea that would be. I was somewhat skeptical but I have to say that the White Mountain idea was presented to us as a question, not a demand, so it seemed safe enough. Marie and I agreed and off we went to White Mountain.

At its highest point, White Mountain is almost 8,000 feet in elevation. I'm not sure if the cowboys wanted to take us to the top of White Mountain or if they had other plans for us but the panic alarm started going off in Marie and I fairly quickly. We became increasingly worried as they drove us, mile after mile, up that mountain. With each passing minute, it seemed less likely that we were going to go dancing that night. Marie and I couldn't really communicate our fears to each other since we were sitting between the two cowboys but it was pretty obvious to both of us that we might be in BIG trouble. So, Marie did the only thing that seemed logical to her at the time; she became hysterical, burst into tears and begged them to return us to Rock Springs! And, I'll be darned if that's not exactly what they did.

They turned around, headed down the mountain, and made no attempts at all to harm us in any way. In fact, once we were down the mountain, we ended up spending the evening with them at their apartment and they were just as harmless as could be. However, the memory of that "What have we gotten ourselves into?" moment up on that mountain remains one of the most dramatic memories of my life.

* * *

After all that drama in Rock Springs, the trip from there to Toledo was fairly uneventful. We had hoped to visit the U.S. Mint in Denver, Colorado but it was closed due to the Labor Day holiday. After the first thousand miles of a road trip, things can become fairly monotonous especially with interstate travelling through states like Kansas and Missouri. It comes as no surprise to me that I have no memories of going through those states except for arriving in St. Louis.

When we arrived in St. Louis, I began to get really excited! We were getting close to home. I saw the highway sign indicating the city of Troy, Illinois, wasn't far away. I can remember singing a little jingle "Troy, oh Troy, we'll be seeing you soon" (meaning my brother, not the city) and I became distracted. The next thing I knew, we accidentally veered off on the wrong road and headed north, on Interstate 55, instead of continuing east on I-70 towards Toledo. After several days on the road, this felt like a catastrophe. I think we drove a good 40-50 miles before we realized our mistake, turned around, and headed to Toledo. My enthusiasm waned.

I was never so happy to see the Cumberland County sign when we finally got closer to home. I'm sure from that point on, I chattered to Marie, giving her various details of my family member's names, ages, status, etc. It was such an exciting thing to be taking a Navy friend to my hometown.

I don't actually remember pulling into the driveway of my parents' home but I do remember the attention my little Toyota garnered once we hit Toledo. It was almost comical. I don't think I could have received more comments than if I had arrived home in an Amish buggy. My little car was a complete oddity in Toledo. But everyone who rode in it agreed that it was a pretty nice little car.

By the time Marie and I hit Toledo, she and I were both getting on each other's nerves. Our visit in Toledo gave us an opportunity to have some space away from each other and regroup for the rest of our journey. Earlier that year, my uncle, John Wilson had visited Las Vegas, Nevada with two of his friends; Alan Ross and Brad Harvey. When they were there on vacation, Marie and I had driven to Las Vegas to see them. Marie and Brad had become acquainted and liked each other so

Marie decided to visit him during this break in our travelling. This also gave me a chance to be alone with my family which I think I needed.

Looking back on it, it seems logical that any two young people cramped up in a little car for 2,000 miles might need a break from each other but I don't think we thought in such simple logical terms. I think we were both too young and assumed it was easily the "other one's" fault if things weren't going well.

Our time in Toledo didn't last long and, too soon, we were back on the road headed towards Virginia. When we left Toledo, we weren't on the best of terms so we drove in silence not speaking to each other. But, as Marie remembers it, someone (probably mom) had given us some barbecue when we left home. We hadn't travelled very far from Toledo when I said to Marie, "Are you hungry?" and we both burst into giggles and dug into the barbecue. That was the fun thing about Marie. She could easily see the humor in any situation and didn't tend to stay mad long.

\* \* \*

The trip to Virginia was very different than our first 2,000 miles when we could basically aim the car in an easterly direction and just drive. Driving to Virginia from Toledo required a little more effort at studying a map and making sure we stayed on all the right roads. All in all, though, that trip seemed very short in comparison to the first part of the trip.

When possible, Marie and I liked using military bases for overnight lodging. When we were travelling together, the military lodges offered us both a safe place to stay as well as an economical room. That was one of the perks of being in the military. So we found an Air Force base to stay in when we drove through Ohio. The lodges at Air Force bases were always the nicest and most modern. The next morning, we woke up and drove on to Virginia.

When we arrived in Virginia, we drove straight to my uncle and aunt's house (H.A. and Brenda Wilson) at Fort Eustis. My uncle, H.A., had been in the army several years and he and his family lived on the Fort Eustis post. H.A. and Brenda had three sons; H.D., Bailey, and Jay. The boys were close in ages to my brothers and were very active in sports during their time in Virginia. Their base was only about 30 miles from where I would be going to school in Norfolk. It would be the only time in my Navy years that I would be stationed so close to family members.

Marie and I stayed overnight at H.A. and Brenda's house before Marie had to leave to fly up to her parents' home in New Hampshire. On our final day together, we decided to become blood sisters. After surviving that 3,000 mile journey together, we felt we should do something special to symbolize our friendship. So we each lanced a finger, making the smallest puncture possible, and then squeezed with all our might to get a single drop of blood out of each of us (such wimps we were). Then, we smeared our blood together and declared ourselves "blood sisters". It probably sounds juvenile but it was something I had always heard of when I was a kid and thought it would be the perfect way for us to declare ourselves something more than just friends.

## Chapter 19

# The Armpit of the World

Upon arrival to Naval Station, Norfolk, Virginia, I was quickly informed that my new base was nicknamed the "armpit of the world" and it didn't take long to figure out why! My base in California had been so beautiful and picturesque. In contrast, the base in Norfolk appeared to be comprised of nothing but old brick buildings, concrete, and asphalt. I had transferred from a world of vibrant color to a world of black and white (and brick red). In California, everything seemed so clean and new. The East Coast, in comparison, seemed old and decrepit. California's highways made sense to me; I was seldom confused when it came to exiting off a highway or getting on to one. The East Coast highways were awful. The roads were in terrible condition compared to California's highways. Many of the off-ramps were somewhat concealed and, therefore, navigation always included some anxiety. During my short time in Virginia, those roads were enough to convince me I never wanted to live in that area of the country again.

Confusion with navigating the highways paled in comparison, though, to the stress I felt from my new environment at Norfolk. On my Navy base in California, the sailors had seemed professional, courteous, and respectful of women. In contrast, the sailors on the base at Norfolk seemed like savages! At Moffett Field, I often jogged around a track behind my barracks and attracted very little male attention. The first week in Norfolk, I attempted jogging on the base and the results were almost traumatizing! I was the subject of horrible "cat calls" and male sailors gawking at me. It was an incredible culture shock.

Within the military, there are all kinds of rivalries (just like in high school or with sports teams). In the Navy, the "Airdales" (military people associated with the aviation part of the Navy) sometimes look down on the "Black Shoes" (people stationed aboard ships). I was beginning to understand why. It was the equivalent of two different subcultures. At Moffett Field, there had been many high tech jobs that required a certain level of intelligence. At Norfolk, I felt surrounded by men who were completely different; many of them were sea-going sailors without the sophistication of the naval aviators I had become familiar with. The Black shoes had a higher percentage of lower skilled jobs (although there were many jobs in both communities that required a high level of intelligence). The Black shoes also spent long periods of time at sea in the presence of males only. Thus, they often reacted more strongly to females when they did get the chance to be around them. Airdales rarely went anywhere there were not females so they seldom went into caveman mode. In Norfolk, I became acutely aware of whose side I was on and it wasn't the "Black Shoes"! They appeared to be immature and have a complete lack of respect for female sailors.

The good news was that I actually had a roommate I liked! Her name was Julie. She was young, cute, blonde and friendly. The room we shared was huge compared to my barracks room at Moffett Field. So, we had plenty of space for ourselves which made a big difference in being comfortable, feeling some sense of privacy, and tolerating each other's quirks. We had a third roommate, a female Marine, but we didn't see much of her. She was a nice girl though and a big improvement over my weird roommates in California.

Julie had grown up in the Catskill Mountains in New York. On one of my weekends during my time in Virginia, Julie and I drove up to her parents' home to spend the weekend. It was beautiful up there but I think I would have thought the same thing of <u>any</u> destination I escaped to from Norfolk!

### Letter from Marie *(my blood sister)*
Undated *(but sent during my first few days at Norfolk while she was still on leave at her parents' home in New Hampshire)*

*Dear Kathy,*

*I miss you more than I've ever missed anyone in my entire life. I feel as though someone cut off my right arm and sent it to Virginia. What does this mean?? Will I be able to continue living in a normal manner upon return to Moffett Field? Will these sleepless nights end — my head dancing with exciting things to tell you?*

*I hate to get dramatic. Send me your phone number as soon as you get one. Miss you terribly.*

*Love, Mame*

# Chapter 20

# My Haven

Within the first two weeks in Norfolk, it became very clear to me that the best part of being stationed in Virginia would be visiting my uncle and aunt, H.A. and Brenda Wilson. I loved escaping Norfolk and going to their house; my Aunt Brenda was a wonderful cook and their home was a complete haven from the dismal environment of the Navy base at Norfolk. Emotionally, visiting their house was as close as I could get to the feeling of being in my parents' or grandparents' homes in Toledo.

I loved all of Brenda's home-cooked meals but the thing I loved most was one of her desserts, "Vanilla Pie". I've made it hundreds of times since those days in Virginia and it remains one of my favorite desserts.

I admired my Aunt Brenda in so many ways. Not only did I think she was the perfect military wife but I admired her ability to make and keep so many good friends, to be such a good mom to her three boys, and to successfully juggle so many activities in her life. No matter how busy she was, she never made me feel like she was too busy to spend time with me or listen to me when I wanted to whine about Norfolk.

## Recipe for Vanilla Pie:

1st Layer:  1 cup flour

1 cup nuts

1 stick oleo

*Mix and spread in 9x13 pan.  Bake 15 mins at 350 degrees. Cool*

2nd Layer:  8 oz. cream cheese

¾ cup powdered sugar

Mix with mixer and spread on first layer.

3rd Layer:  2 small pkgs instant vanilla pudding

2 1/3 cups milk

1 small container cool whip

(use only ½ of container)

Top Layer: Use remaining cool whip

\* \* \*

My schedule at my school on the Norfolk base wasn't bad; I attended classes Monday through Friday and was usually out of school by 3 or 4:00. When my classes were over on Friday afternoons, I would often head to H.A. and Brenda's house. A shopping mall was conveniently located between my base and their base, just off the highway at Newport News, so I occasionally stopped there to do some shopping.

One evening, I went to the mall but didn't arrive until after dark. I liked to shop for greeting cards to send to people and stuffed animals for my barracks room. I was in a gift store, slightly bent over, looking at some stuffed animals on a lower rack. Suddenly, I felt a body rub up against my backside. Startled, I stood up and look around; at first, I thought there hadn't been enough room for the person to get around me but that wasn't the case. The person who had rubbed up against me was a tall African American man and, after that deliberate physical contact, he went over to the entry of the store and stood there as if to wait on me. I thought "Surely, this is my imagination, this can't be happening" so I decided to exit the store and go into a couple other stores to test whether or not he was following me. He followed me to the entrance of both stores and stood there with his eyes locked on me, tracking my every move the entire time I was in both stores. That's when I started to panic.

There was no way I was going to leave the mall and walk out to the parking lot alone. In the third store, I decided to purchase an item. After getting in line to pay for it, a young clean-cut guy got in line behind me. I noticed his Navy style haircut and felt sure he was in the military. So, I struck up a conversation with him. "Are you in the military?" I asked and he said "Yeah, I'm in the Navy." I said "Oh, me too." I asked him where he was stationed and then told him where I was stationed. Feeling a slight amount of rapport with him, I looked into his eyes and said "I think I'm being followed" and asked him to glance over at the entrance of the store where the man was standing. I said "Could you do me a big favor and walk me out to my car? I'm scared to go out alone." He totally got what was happening and said "Sure, no problem."

As we exited the store, the tall man watched us and followed us for a few yards until he realized the sailor was sticking by me. Finally, the stalker walked off in a different direction. Once my Good Samaritan and I neared the mall exit, I thanked him and told him I could walk the rest of the way by myself.

When I arrived at H.A. and Brenda's house later that evening, I told Brenda about this frightening encounter. She said "Kathy, didn't you hear about the series of rapes out there? You should never go to that mall alone at night!" I was stunned and realized I had been correct in my assessment of the stalker.

There have been many times since then that I've thought about that incident. It was such a creepy feeling to be stalked. Simply put, I felt like "prey". There have been few times in my life when I've been that frightened. Unfortunately, I think the trauma of that incident further convinced me I would never want to live in that area of Virginia. For as nice as it was to visit H.A. and Brenda, I was very glad I was only stationed on the east coast for 4 months and not longer.

*Uncle Bob Scott's advice of "remember you're not in Toledo so keep your eyes open" ended up being more relevant than I would have liked it to be.*

## Note left for me in my barracks room by my roommate, Julie.

*December 13, 1978*
*Kathy,*

*Your sister called and would like to wish you a happy birthday. Happy Birthday from me too!*
*Julie*

My school, Ocean Systems Technician "A" School was not easy. In fact, 50 percent of our class flunked the course. I'm sure some of the students probably had no idea what the class was really about when they applied for it. The name of the course/rating, "Ocean Systems Technician" was not very applicable to what we actually did. For sailors new to the Navy who had not had a thorough explanation of what this job would consist of (as I had in the closed-door session at Moffett Field), I'm sure they were more than a little confused to find themselves studying antisubmarine warfare. That's what the school was all about though; it had little to do with oceanography. As an OT, our job would be to detect, track and localize submarines and surface vessels by analyzing the sounds made by engine systems and subsystems.

During the course of my 4-month school, I studied very hard in order to do well. Learning about diesel and nuclear submarines' engine systems and anti-submarine warfare was much like learning a foreign language for me. It became apparent why it had been necessary to score high on my ASVAB test to get into this school. I had never been this academically challenged in my life. My approach to the school was much the same as my approach had always been to math: memorize, memorize, memorize even if I didn't understand what I was memorizing. And it worked! I was so proud of my success in that school.

Near the end of our course, orders for the students were received and announcements were made in class of where each of us would be transferring to. Previously, all of the students had submitted duty preference forms listing three choices of duty stations. I had been forewarned that I would probably not get a great location since I had just spent a year in California. I was advised to put at least one "bad" place on my duty preference form. Even though it was logical that my next duty station should be something less desirable than Moffett Field, I really wasn't prepared for the news of getting orders to Adak, Alaska! I had been in the Navy long enough to know that Adak wasn't just an undesirable duty station but one of the worst in terms of isolation. (It had been my third choice, the "bad" choice.) When that information was given to me in class, I walked out of my classroom, went out to the parking lot, got into my car and took off driving with tears streaming down my face. I don't know what got into me! I was never really a rebel and I could have gotten in trouble for leaving the classroom but I didn't. I'm assuming it's because the instructor knew just what rotten news it was for me to get orders to Adak, Alaska!

Being in California had been enough of a hardship in terms of being far from home but Adak would be like living on a different planet! I knew what that meant; probably no trips home for that year. It did not bode well for my mental health. Homesickness had already been overwhelming at times. I couldn't stand the thought of being so much further from home and so isolated from the civilized world.

* * *

I completed OT "A" school on December 1st, 1978, and then drove to Toledo for a short vacation at home. Marie had made the decision to fly to Illinois to meet me so she could drive back to California with me. Four months earlier, when we parted ways at my aunt and uncle's house, I had no idea if we would ever see each other again. I was thrilled that she had decided to be my travelling partner for the return trip to California. I was still new enough to the Navy that I wasn't sure if any of my Navy friendships would last beyond my enlistment. With hindsight, Marie's willingness to fly to Toledo and drive back to California seems significant; it was somewhat symbolic of our friendship continuing beyond our Navy years.

Our first trip across the United States was so eventful that the second one just didn't compare. I have no memories from that trip at all! Marie and I were cross-country veterans at that point. Going back to California was a piece of cake!

Me and Marie at my parents' house opening Christmas gifts

## Chapter 21

# HOCUS POCUS

After we arrived back in California and I took Marie home, I had one final Navy obligation before moving to Alaska. I was scheduled to attend a class, Oceanographic Advanced Subsystems, which started on January 2nd, 1979. It was only about 3 weeks long and was taught at a small, practically hidden little base, the Naval Facility, Centerville Beach. It was located 300 miles north of my previous duty station, Moffett Field.

Northern California is like a separate state from southern California and has its own unique beauty. I loved northern California. It wasn't nearly as commercial as the southern part of the state. My base was located in a rural location five miles from the nearest town, Ferndale. This area reminded me a little of home because Ferndale was small like Toledo and some of the local people were farmers. It was so quaint, so beautiful, and so much like something you might see in a story book. I felt very lucky to have this incredible respite before moving on to my cold, snowy destination.

The course at Centerville Beach helped to give me an idea of what my job would be like on Adak and it also gave me a chance to spend more time with a couple of the friends I had made in Norfolk. I had met a girl, Joslyn, in OT "A" school and we ended up sharing a room together at Centerville Beach. She was the best roommate I ever had.

Joslyn was from the bayous south of New Orleans, Louisiana, and was pure Cajun. Having never met anyone from that part of the country before, I was intrigued with her accent and her "people". One night before going to bed, we were talking and she told me about one of her more interesting family members, her maternal grandmother. "Mémère" (French for "grandma") believed in witchcraft and had concocted all kinds of potions and cast spells on a variety of people. As we lay in our separate twin beds, Joslyn went into quite a bit of detail talking about Mémère and her interesting ways.

Mémère apparently cast spells on family members and others but not in the traditional *"Bewitched"* sense. Instead, she would wish something out loud and then it seemed to happen. For example, three of her sons were involved in a crime and all three went to prison. One day, Joslyn's father made a comment to his mother-in-law, Mémère, that her three sons deserved their punishment. This was not something Mémère wanted to hear. She then proclaimed loudly that she wished <u>his</u> three sons would all go to jail so that he would understand her pain. Within a month, Joslyn's three brothers were each accused of a different crime and sent to jail!

Mémère was also a healer. In that culture, healers used different methods of healing; they would hold hands on you, say special "prayers", and create "potions" to heal ailments. It was considered white magic. The potions Joslyn's grandmother created were very similar to Eastern medicines. If a family member got stung by an insect, Joslyn's grandmother used wet tobacco and secure it to the affected area. For cuts, she searched and found spider webs and applied them to the injured area. The web would stop the bleeding and help heal the wound. For the flu, she cooked big cockroaches (palmetto bugs) and had the afflicted family member drink the broth. (Yum!) For coughs, she brewed <u>very</u> strong coffee, added some sugar, poured it into a jelly roll pan and made a form of brittle. Family members with a bad cough would suck on small pieces of the brittle to get well.

I had no knowledge or understanding of Cajun people or of their culture. Everything Joslyn told me about Mémère's ways was new to me. I found the stories a little spooky but I was spellbound by Joslyn's dramatic ability to recite them. Even though Joslyn had grown up in that culture, she seemed to be as creeped out by some of her grandmother's activities as I was. At the very least, there was a definite generational and cultural gap between Joslyn and her grandmother.

Despite the thought-provoking conversation, Joslyn and I eventually grew tired and turned the lights out. The next morning, we were both surprised when our phone rang and woke us up. I jumped up and grabbed the phone (the phone being located out of reach on the wall of our barracks room). The caller asked to speak with Joslyn. I indicated to Joslyn that the call was for her and crawled back in bed. I heard Joslyn speaking but mostly in single words; "okay", "yeah", "alright". She hung the phone up, looked over at me with a look of complete shock on her face, and said "Kathy, you won't believe what happened! My grandmother DIED last night!" Chills went through both of us! We looked at each other with a look of utter disbelief. As bizarre as it sounds, Joslyn couldn't help but feel there had been some connection between our discussion of her grandmother the night before and her dying at nearly the same time. This all seemed surreal. It felt like something straight out of an episode of "The Twilight Zone".

But things got even more dramatic for Joslyn. When she flew home for her grandmother's funeral and landed in New

Orleans, her airplane actually skidded off the runway and into a muddy area! Joslyn said she had never been that scared in her entire life. I couldn't help but wonder if Mémère had something to do with that plane skidding off the runway. Maybe she performed a little hocus pocus from her grave.

\* \* \*

After my course ended at Centerville Beach, I had to face one of the worst things about transferring to Alaska; parting with my Toyota. I had made the decision to store my car in California the year I was on Adak. Islands are very hard on cars because of the humid conditions and salt-laden air. I had been advised by numerous Navy friends not to take my car to Adak for those reasons. They all told me it would probably be ruined. So, I placed an ad in the San Jose Mercury and found a woman willing to store my car in her garage for only $50 per month. It was a little scary trusting this complete stranger, Linda, with my precious car but I had no other options. I drove from Centerville Beach down to her house in Sunnyvale, and dropped my car off. Then, a friend gave me a ride to the airport in San Francisco and I flew to Seattle to catch my flight to Adak. During the year I lived in Adak, I called Linda a few times to check on my "baby". She always assured me that my little car was just fine.

# Part Four:
# ADAK, ALASKA
## February 1979- February 1980

## Chapter 22

# 365 Days But Who's Counting?

I had come to terms with my year in exile (that's how I felt about going to Adak) and decided to approach it as yet another adventure. If nothing else, I knew I was embarking on a unique opportunity. Adak is a volcanic island in the Andreanof Island group of the Aleutian archipelago, located almost halfway across the Bering Sea between Alaska and the (then) Soviet Union. It is the westernmost municipality in the United States and the southernmost town in Alaska. Adak has one large mountain, Mount Moffett (ironically), and is home to hundreds of bald eagles.

At that time, I could sum up my knowledge of what island living was like in two words: *Gilligan's Island*. After landing on Adak, it became very apparent to me why those castaways were always scheming of ways to escape their island. I thought quite often about Gilligan, Ginger, Mary Ann, and the millionaire and his wife. In fact, I just bet that on some subliminal level, they taught me a thing or two about adapting and surviving island life.

While Adak was not the most desirable place to be stationed, it had its redeeming qualities. It was a small community with one place to shop, one small library, one gas station, one medical clinic, and a whopping 16 miles of paved and gravel roads! In many ways, it was like living in Toledo. It didn't take long to figure out where everything was, it didn't take long to get acquainted with people there, and it was a cheap place to live because there wasn't much to spend money on (other than flights out of there!).

The Navy made valiant attempts to help with the morale of its sailors and their families on Adak. Decades before I lived there, the Navy brought in a herd of caribou for people to hunt. That, of course, wasn't my thing. In fact, it really wasn't an activity many people could partake of. You had to have the money and resources to go on those caribou hunts (it required taking a boat to the other side of the island and having all the right equipment for such an expedition). Very few people participated in that activity although there were sailors who asked for orders to Adak for that specific reason. Some of those outdoorsmen even volunteered to stay in Adak for a second tour of duty.

For anyone not familiar with the Navy, there are acronyms galore. Within any Navy Base, there are usually a variety of "commands" which refers to separate entities located on the Navy base. The Naval Facility (NavFac) I worked at had a secret mission of detecting and locating Soviet submarines so that P-3's flying from Adak could locate them. The entire population of workers/employees at a NavFac consisted of about 150 people.

The Naval Air Station (NAS) was built to support three different commands: the NavFac, the Naval Security Group Activity (NSGA), and the deployed VP Squadrons. The NSGA had a mission of intercepting Soviet radio communications and the VP Squadrons flew daily antisubmarine warfare (ASW) missions and intelligence gathering flights off the coast of Russia. Everyone else on the island filled a support role to the three organizations directly involved in fighting the Cold War. At the peak of the Cold War, there were 6,000 Navy and Coast Guard personnel, their families, and civilian contractors living at NAS Adak.

* * *

Upon my initial arrival to Adak and getting settled in my barracks room, I heard a knock on my door. When I opened the door, I was pleasantly surprised to see a very cheerful and friendly young woman welcoming me to Adak. She introduced herself as "Maureen" and handed me an Adak "Short-timer's calendar"; a piece of 8x10 white paper with the shape of Adak divided into 365 blocks. Maureen explained that I should color in, one at a time, each of the 365 blocks representing the days I would spend on the island. This was a real bonding moment for me and Maureen. Once I had that short-timer's calendar in hand, I felt like I was a true citizen of Adak.

Within five minutes of talking to Maureen, I no longer felt new in the way most people would at a new base. We were instant friends. This single welcoming gesture of hers would make a tremendous difference in my adjustment to Adak. Unlike Moffett Field, where it took me a few weeks to feel like I fit in, Maureen helped me to feel like Adak was home the very first week!

My barracks room was small, a 9 or 10-foot square box with one window. I had a bunk bed, a closet, and one other piece of furniture. As I recall, the floor was a dark tile and the walls were painted a cream color; a typical and unremarkable military color scheme. The best thing about my room, though, was what it did <u>not</u> have ... roommates! I was tickled pink to have a room to myself.

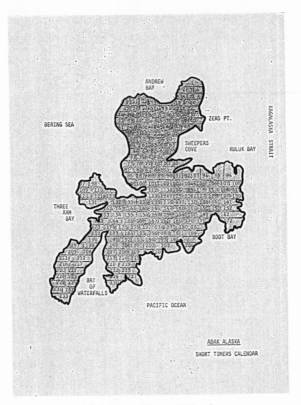

Adak Short-Timers Calendar

It wasn't long before I knew lots of people. I lived in the upstairs of a barracks where many other females lived; the building was a long rectangular building with one long hallway leading to all the rooms the females lived in. Most of us had private rooms but we had to share a large communal bathroom. Things were extremely relaxed with regard to visitors and it wasn't unusual to see men in our barracks visiting their girlfriends and/or staying all night with them. There was virtually no security. While it could be a little annoying and slightly embarrassing to walk to and from the communal bathroom in our robes, encountering men along the way, I don't remember ever feeling unsafe.

There was absolutely nothing modern about the barracks or any of the other buildings located on Bering Hill. The enlisted club, the library, the chow hall, and a couple other buildings were also located there and many of these buildings were connected by an underground tunnel (sort of like a subway but without a train). During winter weather, we always used the tunnel to go from one building to another. Whoever created that tunnel really knew what they were doing. It made life much easier for all of us who lived on "the hill".

## Letter sent from the Commanding Officer of the Adak Naval Facility *to my parents:*
18 February 1979

*Dear Mr. & Mrs. Wilson,*

*I would like to take this opportunity to give you an overview of Naval Facility, Adak, Alaska and let you know a little about what aspect of the Navy your daughter is involved in while stationed here.*

*Since World War II, the U.S. Navy has sought to increase its' knowledge of the ocean environment and information concerning oceanographic and acoustic conditions off the continental coasts. It became apparent during the war that the U.S. lacked information on ocean areas of the Atlantic and Pacific. Consequently, the U.S. Navy has maintained a continuing program of oceanographic surveys and research designed to provide more detailed information of currents, temperature, salinity, and other factors which comprise the oceanic environment and affect the transmission of sound in water. It has been found that one of the most expeditious and economical methods of analyzing certain data is through acoustical hydrophones planted off* shore in the ocean. This data is then fed back to shore based terminals at Naval Facilities, such as the one here on Adak, for analysis. Research has shown that, depending on size, shape and speed, each source emanates its' own sound pattern. By learning more about these sound patterns and determining their source, man-made or natural, the Navy is able to better understand its' operational environment.

The U.S. Naval Facility, Adak, Alaska is situated on the shore of Kuluk Bay at the Northwestern end of Adak, Island. Adak Island, the largest of the Andreanof Islands, is located close to the center of the Aleutian Islands chain, about 1200 miles west of Anchorage, Alaska. The island has a population of around 5,000 people which includes military, dependents, and civilian contractors and dependents. The temperatures on Adak range from a low of 20 to a high of 65 degrees. Winds in the winter months frequently gust to over 50 knots making the chill factor considerably less. There are frequent minor earthquakes on Adak. The length of daylight hours on Adak ranges from 7 hours in the winter to 17 hours in the summer.

There are approximately 150 men and women assigned to this Naval Facility. They are all highly skilled in fields that include electronics and computers as well as clerical personnel and diesel engine maintainers. Over 100 wives and children have accompanied their spouses to Adak and enjoy the numerous indoor and outdoor recreation activities available.

I hope this gives you a general idea of what your daughter is involved in here in the Naval Facility and a little bit about Adak Island. As Commanding Officer of this facility, I am personally committed to insuring the welfare and satisfaction of our men and women. If I can be of any assistance, feel free to contact me or my Executive Officer at any time.

Sincerely yours.
W.E. Inman

The Naval Facility I worked at was located several miles (a 10-15 minute drive) from my barracks. Most of the people who lived in the barracks didn't have their own transportation so we depended on our "chauffeur" to take us to and from work every day. The person serving as our chauffeur differed from day to day; it was one of several different Seabees (men who worked in the construction battalion). Besides their normal jobs on Adak, some of the Seabees had an extra duty of driving us to and from work. We all loved the Seabees! The drivers were young guys that lived in our barracks so we saw them during off-duty hours as well as on our trips to and from work.

Our "taxi" was a white 15-passenger Chevy Van and I marveled at its ability to start up any time of the day or night no matter how cold it was or how severe the weather. Sometimes, our Seabee driver had the van warmed up for us but not all the time. However, with all our bodies squished together, it didn't take long to warm up. On our morning trips to the Navfac, for the day shift, we were usually quiet because we were half-awake. But on our trips after a shift and/or going to work for a night shift, we were often animated and talkative. It wasn't unusual for our Seabee driver to get us stirred up over some comment, story, or joke. Our Seabee drivers were all wonderful guys with great personalities.

The NavFac I worked in had various rooms and departments/divisions within it but the "heart" of the building was the large room I worked in. It was centrally located in the middle of the building and could only be accessed through two different locked doors requiring keyed-in combinations for unlocking. It had little color (mostly drab-gray), no windows, and was filled with the constant noise/drone of the acoustic recording equipment I worked with.

My coworkers and I used a system called SOSUS (Sound Surveillance System) which utilized underwater listening devices for tracking Soviet submarines (I can write about this now because the system was declassified in 1991). Initially, I felt rather inept at using it. As is often the case with formal classroom learning, it doesn't always equate with "real world" knowledge; even though I had successfully completed my "A" school, the reality of analyzing data at the NavFac was a whole different matter. I had to interpret groupings of squiggly lines on long rolls of white paper (which slowly rolled upward as paper does on a desk calculator) on 20 different pieces of recording equipment. It was sort of like an EKG but the lines were not nearly as well-defined. It was very confusing. I had to analyze this data, using algebraic formulas, to determine if the lines were representative of ships, submarines, or other sounds. (The SOSUS equipment actually picked up dolphin and whale "communication" in addition to everything else.) My initial impression of this data was that it just looked like a big black and white mess!

### *Letter from Brenda (Whitaker) Wilson* (my aunt)
February 18, 1979

*Dear Kathy,*

*We enjoyed hearing from you. Glad you survived the vacation at home and the training in California. How is Adak? I'm sure you'll like it. A hardship area generally brings a group closer together.*

*H.A. left on January 2ⁿᵈ and made it over okay {to Germany}. He was there a week, then went out "in the field" for 3 weeks, which was an experience. There was 19 inches of snow on the ground and it was around zero degrees all the time so he nearly froze. He said he learned a lot and thinks he'll enjoy the job. It's a lot different than the job he had and he was ready for a change. So was I.*

*Things have slowed down a lot since football ended. H.D. is playing basketball but Jay and Bailey are taking a break. Baseball starts March 10, so the break is about over. We have about 6 inches of snow on the ground now and it's about 10 degrees -- so it will have to warm up some before they start.*

*Jay has won 2 art contests since you were here and is entering another. We have to go down to New Market North Mall Tuesday night so he can be given an award. It's really hard living with a budding young artist sometimes – he really takes himself seriously.*

*Bailey gets his braces on the second week in March so he's looking forward to that. Somehow they equate it with being a teenager so that makes it worth the hassle.*

*I'm really enjoying my jobs. I supervise 10 student teachers in Speech Pathology, teach one course and then work at the hospital 2 days a week. I work at the hospital from 9:00-1:00 on Tuesday and Thursday and go to Old Dominion University from 9:00-3:00 Monday and Friday and from 1:00-3:00 on Wednesday mornings at home so I'm actually pretty busy.*

*The semester ends April 30 so then I'll just have the hospital until time we leave.*

*I'm enjoying my solitude very much but will be ready to go to Germany in June. I'll probably take the kids home for a week in March so we can't go home over Easter. I get the first week in March off from ODU {Old Dominion University} for Spring Break so I'm looking forward to that.*

*I made Vanilla Pie today and thought of you.*

*I'm enclosing a picture from H.A.'s promotion party. It's not great of you but got you a copy anyway.*

*Hope things are well with you. Write when you get a chance.*

*Love,*
      *Brenda and boys*

## Letter from Susan James *(my former art teacher)*
February 20, 1979

*Dear Kathy,*

*Haven't been able to sleep tonight so have busied myself making jello salads, macaroni salads, cleaning house, etc. But now I have a half hour before getting Shannon up for school and I can't think of a better way to pass it than writing one of my favorite people.*

*I did some illuminated manuscript bible verses for the church a couple of weeks ago, and have done an ink drawing of geese and ducks for my brother-in-law. I haven't gotten to finish my stained glass window as my studio (garage) got a might chilly to work in. It shouldn't take me too many hours to finish it up once the weather begins cooperating. That's about it for my current art projects.*

*I'd like to think spring is definitely coming. In fact, I went out and bought 10 packets of flower seeds to help it along which may be the reason it turned cold again. I've certainly gotten spoiled down here with the warmer weather. Wonder how you're adjusting to your new climate? Also, what does a girl do with her free time up there? My ordinary household projects must seem pretty dull to you.*

*I'd say you had quite a scenic drive from coast to coast. I know it was beautiful and inspiring but somewhat exhausting too. You've seen places most of your friends can't even imagine. Sounds like your family is doing fine but they were happy to have you home in December. Has distance really killed your most recent romance? Or, have you already found an interesting replacement or two?*

*March is Youth Art Month – suppose CJHS & CHS is celebrating? Hope so.*

> *Take care.*
> *As always, Susan*

\* \* \*

I constantly questioned the wisdom of my decision to leave Moffett Field. I had been enveloped in such a supportive group of people there. In my new workplace, I experienced none of that. I felt very much like I was on my own and was, at times, completely miserable. In retrospect, I realize that there was just so much to adjust to. I worked what was referred to as a 2, 2, 2 and 80 schedule. This meant I worked 2 day shifts, then 2 midnight shifts, then two evening shifts and was off for 3 days (80 hours). I liked the 80-hours-off part but hated not having set days off every week and could barely tolerate those midnight shifts. They were brutal.

And if I wasn't real happy, well trust me, there were many others that felt the same way or worse. I never heard any of the people in my rating talking about loving their job. It was quite the opposite. I think many of us thought the "grass would be greener" doing about anything else than what we were doing. At least, I think that's how the females felt. The males knew they were lucky to have non-shipboard jobs and probably were more grateful for their work environment than the females.

Among the many things I didn't enjoy about my new environment, the uniform I had to wear was near the top of the list. At Moffett Field, I had worn my dress uniform every day. While it's not exactly designer clothing, it was a big step up from dungarees. The dungaree uniform consisted of blue jeans and a light blue chambray button-down shirt. The blue jeans didn't look nor feel like good quality blue jeans and the entire uniform seemed much more appropriate attire for prison than the Navy (unless you worked onboard a ship). As if the uniform wasn't bad enough, I had to wear my hair up in an old-lady bun. (I had let my hair grow during the year I was in California.) And looking bad wasn't the worst of it; I was almost always cold at work so I normally kept my army green military-issued parka on throughout the entire day/night of work.

I had had such a perfect life at Moffett Field but had failed to realize it. At that beautiful base in California, I had been blessed with perfect daytime hours, a perfect climate, an extraordinary variety of interesting people, and many encouraging and supportive friends. Plus, I had had my buddy, Marie. In California, I also had my Toyota and access to all kinds of adventure!

In Adak, I felt like a prisoner. It was as if all my freedoms were gone. I had horrible working hours with no option of changing them, cold and dreary conditions in my workplace, cold and dreary conditions OUTSIDE the workplace, and a feeling of isolation you just can't imagine unless you've ever lived in a place like that.

# Toledo Democrat to the Rescue!

I quickly discovered on Adak that letter mail and packages would be just as crucial to my morale as they had been during my time in boot camp. With 365 days to survive on that island, I had plenty of time to ponder and implement creative ideas with letter-writing.

On a particularly boring day in Adak, I fired off a letter to Grandma Olive joking that I wished I could put an ad in the local newspaper, the Toledo Democrat, about a homesick girl wanting cookies sent to her. This, I'm sure, was just a little strategy to get my grandmothers and mom to send me some cookies but Grandma Olive took it a step further. She actually placed an ad in the Toledo Democrat and oh boy -- did I ever receive cookies!

When I lived in the barracks, I missed being able to bake cookies. During my childhood, I often baked cookies with my Aunt Joyce (I think I ate more cookie dough than cookies though) and when I got older, I loved making cookies for my family. Growing up in a family of five children, I had several grateful recipients of my baking efforts.

Grandma Olive's effort resulted in one of the highlights of my year in Adak. Several family members made and mailed homemade cookies to me. Unfortunately, many of the cookies arrived broken up and in crumbs but it didn't matter. It was so much fun receiving, opening, and sharing those boxes of cookies.

Used with permission of Toledo Democrat

## *Letter from Mom* (*not dated but from this timeframe*)

*Kathy,*

*The ad in the Democrat is going to get you a lot of homemade cookies.*

*The snow is gone and it's beginning to look like spring (Thank God). This winter has been harder on my nerves than anything in awhile.*

*Scott & Judy's wedding was real nice. We went with Janet & Richard, then went out to supper with them.*

*Troy has been having a lot of trouble with his allergies and has missed a lot of school.*

*This pen is smearing so I hope you can read this.*

*Love, Mom*

*Everyone enjoys your nice long letters. As you know, long letters are an impossibility for me to write.*

## Letter from Joyce (Scott) Coleman *(my aunt)*
*March 1979*

*Dear Kathy,*

*I am making a real attempt to write frequently or on a more regular basis. I have many times thought "it's too bad Kathy is not aware I'm thinking of her today". For some reason, sitting down with pen and paper is difficult to squeeze in some days. I'm just finishing up two classes. The one class has probably been the most difficult I've ever taken. I would be interested in knowing the number of hours I've devoted to it. I'm sure I'll end up taking more. Education in the form of classes is one of my favorite means of recreation!*

*I did hear from your mom it was not your idea to put the article in the newspaper. Perhaps that means you're not as homesick as I thought.*

*Joyce*

\* \* \*

Something wonderful happened after I had been on Adak a few months – Spring! What a surprise it was to see the island come to life. It was beautiful. The tundra became a magnificent green and it was very spongy. That's when I discovered tundra-stomping (walking/hiking in the tundra). I marveled at the beauty of the island and loved to roam around in the tundra. However, I never ventured too far from the barracks on those tundra stomps because I had two fears. I had been told that you could actually fall deep into recessed areas where the tundra disguised the hollowed out ground underneath. That scared me to death. If I disappeared, I had no idea who would come looking for me or how long it would take before anyone discovered I was even gone. My other fear was simply wandering too far out in the tundra and getting lost. There were no trees to speak of on Adak (except for a teeny tiny group of evergreens comically referred to as the "Adak National Forest") and few landmarks other than the occasional Quonset hut.

One of the things I loved about Adak was the lack of billboards, street signs, clutter, etc. Living there in the late 1970s could not have been much different than living there 30 or 40 years earlier. Most of the island was untouched by modern civilization.

## *Letter from Jeanie Wilson* *(my aunt)*
### *(Spring 1979)*

*Dear Kathy,*

*Your last note makes your little island sound like a paradise retreat away from the hustle and bustle of the world. I am glad you do like it there; it would be a horrible year if you couldn't stand it at all. One must adjust, they say --- however, it seems I spend all my time adjusting – just once I would like something to adjust to me!!*

*I brought the kids to work with me today. The girl I work with has two children so my kids played at her house this morning after I had their pictures taken and we took them to lunch this afternoon. If this spring vacation is any indication of what this summer is going to be like (adjusting) trying to work and coping with things, I don't know if I even want to try to make it.*

*Max is getting so busy this time of year. Everyone wants everything right now or a day ago! He puts in a full day and quite frequently goes back out at night to do paperwork or just get some new piece of machinery ready to be delivered. They are having such a time getting merchandise delivered as they can't get the big transport out on the country roads yet. Still too tore up from winter.*

*Michelle is changing more and more every day. I guess my little girl is gone and my little boy sure isn't far behind. It is so interesting to watch them grow – I look at her and think "Did I really produce and shape that? Then, too, I often wonder – where in the heck did she get that? Not from me!!" One just hopes one does the right things by them and for them.*

*Better close – take care of yourself, Kathy.*

*Thinking of you.*
*Jeanie*

## *Letter from Troy* (age 11)
4-2-79

*Dear Kathy,*

*How are you? I am fine. I liked the picture you sent me. Is your new animal a monkey or a dog?* [stuffed animal]

*Tom Rooney is building on to the church. He is putting in a place to eat, a kitchen, and a library. This will be in one big room. He also redone the entry on the front of the church. This will cost around 35,000 dollars. So there will be a building fund Sunday every week for a while. Mom and Dad put in 1000 dollars. Eric, Scott and I have been saving our money. We are each putting 6 dollars in the building fund. I got in a fight and got a black eye. I am going to send you a picture of it in my next letter.*

*Scott built a pinewood derby in Cub Scouts and got second place in his den. He got a red ribbon and is going to send you a picture of him, his car, and his ribbon.*

*I am in track, I throw the shot and disc. I can throw the shot about 25 feet. I can throw the disc about 70 feet. Mr. Crane says I will do pretty good.*

*It is supposed to snow tonight but I don't think it will.*

*Dad bought me and Scott new bicycles. They are pretty nice.*

*The Bad News Bears are on T.V. once a week now. They are real funny.*

*I went to a sock hop Friday but I didn't feel like dancing that much so I just sat around with Mike Roberts and we just talked and told jokes.*

*Christy finally had a baby. It's a girl. Her name is Kylee Laine Ervin. Well, that's all I have to say. Talk to you later.*

*Bye,*
    *Troy*

Troy stuck to his word and mailed me this picture:

# Letter from Grandma Virginia:
*April 16, 1979*

*Dear Kathy,*

*We missed you at Easter Dinner yesterday but hope you had a good dinner. All of our family, Grandma and Aunt Dot were here for dinner.*

*I thought I mailed your brownies in time for you to get them for Easter but Susie said it took longer than I allowed so guess you will have them late. Tell me the truth how they arrived—if they were stale or not. If there is something you like, tell me.*

*Thursday nite, they had a retirement dinner for me at the Dutch Pantry. Grandad didn't think he felt like going so your mother went with me. They had a real good dinner...ham. Joe gave me a dozen long-stemmed roses. The office gave me a necklace; emerald set with 6 little diamonds around it and a bracelet with my name on one side and on the back "18 years of service Country Companies". And they gave me 2 weeks of vacation pay which I didn't expect. I was really surprised. Don't know if they were glad to get rid of me or really appreciated what I had done. Susie (McMechan) said she went home and cried. She is afraid of who they will hire and that can be bad. Susie and I did have a good working relationship. That is life...you just have to go on. This is my 3$^{rd}$ week off and I really haven't missed it at all. This is a good time of year to retire as there is so much to do.*

*Grandad is to get his glasses this week. I sure hope he can see to get around. His arthritis is bothering him so much, but maybe with better weather, it will be better. He has stayed pretty cheerful, but not being able to see since Jan. 2, is a long time. We go some place every day.*

*So-long for now.*

*Love,*
*Grandma*

## *Letter from Jeanie Wilson* (*my aunt*)
*May 11, 1979*

*Dear Kathy,*

*Well, two days in the fields and then rain. Not a flooding storm but enough to stop things a bit.*

*I am planning to have all over for Mother's Day to cook-out. It may be just your folks and the grandparents, as Alice and Phil have a tournament in Memphis, but your folks may go down there too. So, at this time, it is who ever may come!! We will miss you there as we do at all our gatherings.*

*Thank you for your lovely letter. Things like that really perk one up and give you a new view of yourself. That came at a very good time – you must have known and planned it that way. Thanks again.*

*This is short, but sweet. I'll write longer later – just wanted to send you this card.*

*I'm sure you do miss having someone to date but perhaps someone else will be stationed there you get to know and like quite soon.*

*Take good care of yourself – and be good.*

> *Thinking of you,*
> *Jeanie*

### Letter FROM ME *to my parents*

This letter is undated but it must have been written in the middle or near the end of my year on Adak. I certainly didn't feel like this all the time but this letter is symbolic of just how monotonous and boring life on a tiny island can be.

*Dear Mom & Dad,*

*I'm so tired of being bored and grouchy. That's how it's been now for about a solid week. I'm going to go absolutely stark-raving mad if things don't change soon. How much can a person take??*

*I tried to expand myself intellectually by going to the Adak museum Sunday. Sure, it was interesting but I had seen practically everything there 20 minutes after I entered the place.*

*I jumped rope and bought a "Mademoiselle" magazine. The two, combined, entertained me for all of a ½ hour. Then, I watched Adak's only soap opera, General Hospital. I probably could have done without that.*

*I'm contemplating taking a shower now. Somehow though, I'm afraid that's not going to do anything for me either.*

*I don't even feel like going for a walk. I'm so tired of looking at Adak; I want to look at trees, buildings that are more than 2 stories high, crowded highways with beautiful cars, horses, cows, motorcycles, civilian houses, "McDonald's", and I'd even settle for a John Deere tractor pulling a plow behind it. Anything different.*

*After pondering over the subject of boredom for the past 10 minutes, I've decided what I'm going to do. I'm going to take a shower and go to the movie. The only problem is it's 4:35 and the movie starts at 7:30. I have a funny feeling my plans won't completely get rid of the boredom, but anything's better than sitting in this room rotting away.*

*I'll write more later (hopefully a bit more cheery)!*

*Love, Kathy*
*p.s. Thanks gobs for the Democrat & upcoming Democrats!*

The day I wrote that letter would have been the kind of day when I would have reflected back on my year at Moffett Field (the good ole days) and wondered why I ever left that utopia!

There are so many things that can be difficult about being stationed in a place like Adak and boredom was definitely near the top of the list.

# Chapter 24

# Marcus

Despite the details of my boredom in the previous letter, I have very fond memories of many good times on Adak. Shortly after arriving on Adak, one of the girls in my barracks took me to a fellow sailor's room and introduced me to "Marcus". The NavFac guys' barracks was located next to the female barracks so we were like next-door neighbors. Marcus and I hit it off that very first night. He was not like the other guys. He was, in a word, gay. The "don't ask, don't tell" policy in the Navy protected Marcus as long as he didn't declare he was gay. He was well-liked and he never openly talked about his sexuality so no one seemed to care. At that point in time, even though it seemed quite obvious to <u>me</u> that he was gay, I don't think he had fully come to terms with it yet.

Marcus was quite effeminate; not only was it obvious in his physique and his mannerisms but also in his interests. He loved to crochet. In some ways, he was more like a little old lady than a young sailor. The first time I visited him, he crocheted the entire time I was there. He had a wild side though. He loved to cuss (just to shock me) and was pretty out-spoken in some ways.

Being with Marcus was like being eight years old again and playing make-believe. At some point in our time in Adak, he decided we should both have soap opera names. (We both watched the island's only soap opera, *General Hospital* and loved to talk about it.) He became "Derek" and I became "Kamisha".

Marcus was so much fun. We had so many good laughs together! Up to that point in my enlistment, no one (except Marie) had felt as much like family as Marcus did.    For me, Marcus was like having a best friend, grandma, and brother all wrapped into one person. He and I spent hours and hours together in his room, talking, laughing, gossiping, and watching TV.

Marcus had divided his room into two sections; a small living room and a bedroom.  (The guys' barracks also had a communal restroom.)  In his living room, I felt just as at home as I would in my grandma's living room. He had a living room couch which was a luxury for a barracks room. He draped a purple knitted afghan over the back of it which helped his room to have a very cozy atmosphere. He also had a homemade entertainment center with a large TV on it.

The barracks on Adak were unique in that we were allowed to do about anything we wanted to fix up and decorate our rooms.  Some of the guys actually went out into the tundra and gathered wood from old World War II Quonset huts and used the wood for making bunk beds, cabinets, entertainment centers, etc. It was amazing how creative those guys were!  Of course, we had a contingent of Seabees on the island so it was pretty easy to find a Seabee to help with small construction projects.

If Marcus and I weren't in his living room watching TV and talking, we were out at the enlisted club dancing together. We loved going to the club because we loved the disco music of that time.  Practically every Friday and Saturday night (at least the nights I wasn't working), we walked down to the club and that's where we spent our evening. We danced up a storm. The song, "We are Family", can take me back to that time in a heartbeat!

I remember showing up at Marcus' room one night and he was so happy because he had received a blue satin shirt in the mail. He had ordered it just for our nights out at the club. Marcus was constantly concerned about his appearance. He was too thin and would go on eating binges to try to gain weight. He also worried about his complexion and often tried new ointments to improve it. He had had a serious case of acne when he was younger and had scars from it. All in all, Marcus really wasn't a handsome guy but his personality more than made up for it.

I don't remember having any boyfriends that first couple of months in Adak and I'm sure it was because Marcus and I were always together.

# Chapter 25

# Letters, Wonderful Letters..

I liked dancing at the club, I liked going tundra-stomping, and I liked spending time with Marcus but nothing quite compared to getting a good letter from home when I was on Adak. Many years later, I still love the letters I received and treasure each and every one of them.

## Letter from Eric  (age 15, almost 16)
*Postmarked June 14, 1979*

*Kathy,*

*I only had one picture left on my roll of film so here is one picture. I will send you a couple more better shots later.*

*I think it will be a nice car. I got a new tape player & speakers for it. I am trying to fix it up real nice. I will have to get a couple of more things for it and it will be all ok and complete. I will probably get something else to drive for good gas mileage. Whatever it is, it will be cheap. If you are wondering what I need for my birthday, I could use a lot of $$ (money). ha ha*

*I will write you again soon. It is getting late and I am tired. Bye.*

*Eric Wilson*

*p.s. I hope you are not lonesome. Farming wore me out and I never got caught up on my sleep. Bye*

## Letter from Rita (Brandenburg) Swearingen
*When this letter was written, Rita was married to my uncle, Monty Swearingen*

*June 21, 1979*

*Dear Kathy,*

*I'm sorry I didn't get back to you until now but it's been a busy week. I'm glad you enjoyed the letter and keep up the quick replies. I'll get back to you as soon as I can. Some weeks I sit in this office and do nothing but kill flies and search for something to read; other weeks, I'm so busy, I hardly have time to breathe.*

*Kathy, don't feel bad about your friends not writing because they get occupied with kids, work, and all the other things in everyday life. It seems to me that I hardly ever think about my school friends unless I happen to see them out somewhere. We all get caught up in the rat race of business.*

*Monty and I make our living for a whole year thru the summer; that means no vacations until it's cold and then where can you go? I think I'd like to see Montana, Wyoming and Colorado sometime when it's warm. Maybe we can take our snowmobile and go when it's cold.*

*As far as you being the only single one at your first class reunion, consider yourself the only smart and the luckiest one out of the whole bunch. Just think about all the laundry you'd be doing for him and besides that, you'd have to wait on him hand and foot. I'll tell you that gets old <u>fast</u>!*

*Let me tell you about my week. First, we had another Swearingen reunion. Sunday was Father's Day, you know. So we had a cookout at Lytle Park in Mattoon. We and Pat & Don took our gas grills and made hamburgers, hot dogs, and barbeque chicken. Boy, was it <u>delish</u>! Afterward, some of us went swimming. David jumped in where it was too deep and the lifeguard had to pull him out but we all had a good time. Susie came up and we were all glad to see her. We are hoping we can do it again the 4<sup>th</sup> of July.*

*Grandma Foote died Tuesday. She had been in the hospital for a few days because she had hardening of the arteries and she was kinda out of her head so they decided she wasn't safe to be alone and must go to a nursing home. She was there at the Mattoon Health Center two days and died. She was happy there though because she told them the last day she was there that she really liked it. She was almost 89. Visitation is tonight and the funeral is tomorrow, Friday, at*

*2:00. She's so much better off because she could hardly hear and she couldn't see and was getting so mixed up. It's better to go like that than to lay and suffer a long time. It's going to be kind of hard on Grandma Swearingen because she has been staying every other week with her because she was afraid to stay alone. You know when you're with someone that often, you can really get close.*

*Sunday, Duane, Carolyn, their kids, and Monty & I are going to Six Flags. Lisa is going to keep Matt. I think that would be too much walking for him.*

*Well, I better get to work on yesterday's accounts receivable. Write soon.*

*Love, Rita*
*P.S. I always heard Alaska was cold. What is the average temp?*

One of the most incredible things that happened when I was in Adak was that two of my great-grandmothers died just a week apart from each other and their obituaries were side-by-side in the newspaper. I had not known my Great-grandma Foote but had grown up near my Great-grandma Scott. While I couldn't make it home in time for Grandma Scott's funeral, I decided to take emergency leave and go home anyway (arriving after her funeral had already taken place). I knew it would be good for me to have a break from life on Adak.

Grandma Scott died on June 27, 1979. I called Moffett Field from Adak trying to get a hop to Moffett so it wouldn't cost as much to fly home. I talked to a Navy man in charge of scheduling the flight. A few months later, we met each other and somehow realized we had talked to each other on the phone at that earlier point in time. Amazingly, that man eventually became my husband.

\* \* \*

It's always a morale booster to move up in rank. After being on Adak a few months, I advanced in rank to Ocean Systems Technician 3rd Class. Master Chief Johnson, from Moffett Field, happened to visit Adak about this time. We were able to see each other and chat but I don't think the results had come out until after his visit. Once he found out I had made Petty Officer Third Class, he sent me this letter to congratulate me:

## Letter from Master Chief Johnson
6 July 1979

Dear _Petty Officer_ Swearingen:

CONGRATULATIONS! I read about you being "frocked" in your Adak paper. It was good to see you when I was up there for the Change of Command; too bad we didn't have longer to talk.

You know it's not my policy to twist anybody's arm to stay in my Navy but I want you to really give it serious thought. By no means let peer pressure have anything to do with your finally making up your mind! It's your life, and your decision to make in the end, so never mind what any of your shipmates think about it. I believe you will do well in the Navy if you decide to stay in.

Enough preaching from me. I've got work to do... so will close. Again congratulations on making 3rd class, now get to work on 2nd!

Best regards,
C. R. Johnson
NCCM    USN

\* \* \*

In the years I moved around in the Navy (I lived in 6 different places within 4 years), my Aunt Brenda was a huge inspiration to me. She had already been a military wife for quite some time when I joined the Navy and I really admired her for her positive attitude and efficiency at dealing with all the things you have to deal with when you move every 2-3 years. She sent the following letter to me shortly after she and her sons moved to Germany to join her husband, H.A., where he was stationed.

## *Letter from Brenda Wilson* (in Germany)
*Postmarked July 31, 1979*

*Dear Kathy,*

*Hope you enjoyed your trip home – sorry we missed you and was sorry about your grandma's death. We enjoyed going home & was glad to see everyone but was in such a state of disorientation; just too much on my mind. Clearing a post & arranging for an overseas move by yourself is no fun - don't know if I'd do it again. I did have a lot of help and Fran and Eileen had a going-away party for me and we had lots of dinner invitations the few weeks before I left. Also, the kids in the neighborhood brought me flowers and had a going-away party for the boys. It was all very nice and I hated to leave. I sold my car with no problem and got what I wanted for it. The gas crunch helped; everyone with a big car was looking for a smaller one.*

*Getting here was a big adjustment as I'm sure Adak was for you; big time and climate difference and different driving laws. I had to study 10 hours for my driving test but passed the first time. Bailey got his braces on before I left. Have been getting arranged here as far as H.D.'s ears and Bailey's teeth and allergies, etc. School registration is next week.*

*I'm checking into jobs here but don't know what the prospects are yet. We're in temporary quarters at Hanau and will move to Gelnhausen in a few weeks. It takes about 2 months for your things to arrive from the states so living here is pretty basic for now. I bought all the kids school clothes before I left so hope they arrive before school starts. Drop a line when you get a chance.*

*Brenda*

## Letter from Grandma Olive
*August 13, 1979*

*Dear Kathy,*

*Sorry I've been so slow writing. I guess the high temperatures slowed me down. It is cooler now and I am very thankful.*

*We had a nice weekend at Louisville Downs, Kentucky races. Ben didn't win but we enjoyed the races anyhow. We stayed overnight and went to Evansville and visited Harold & Eloise and families. Ruth Ann and Sharon were there with their children. Your folks came and Troy and Scott. I guess Troy's horse Charlie got for him got his leg broken. I told him he could get another one. He hadn't had this one very long so he wasn't attached to it so much.*

*I'm staying at the store for Vera for a day or two while they are gone on a little vacation. The big rains about ruined our gardens. Sweet corn is ready so I'll put some in the freezer and Alice is doing it today. Pap is helping her husk it. I put up several sweet pickles and some zucchini relish. The beans got soft & spoiled and the potatoes rotted in the ground.*

*John McKinley is very poorly. They think he may have Legionaires Disease.*

*Do you hear from Brenda? She said they were getting adjusted somewhat. The boys were doing better than she was. Their household things had not arrived yet.*

*The new room is done on the church. I'll take some pictures and send them when I get time. I hope we use it a lot. We got our preacher back again. We are thankful.*

*I hear your Grandad Bill is improving some. Our 50th Class Reunion is Saturday at the Dutch Pantry. I hope he is able to come. Judy thought he might.*

*School is going to start soon. It doesn't seem possible. Fall is about here.*

*John Sowers went into the hospital for gall stone surgery today. John Wilson is taking his place on the state job.*

*Jenny has moved to Brownstown near Vandalia. She has to change schools and she is worried about it. I think she will come up next week for a few days and go to the fair.*

*The Fall Festival will be here before we know it. Then winter. I dread it. I hope we don't have a fuel shortage.*

*I think Eric has his car torn up. I guess he is following in his dad's footsteps. Ha ha*

*Jeanie is about as usual; I don't think she has quite so many headaches. Her kids are coming home for the winter after staying with their dad through the summer.*

*Max is busy helping get the Fairground in good condition for the races and the crowds.*

*Phil hit his 40th home run the other night. Alice is helping with the Little Miss Queens again this year.*

*A very nice amusement place has been opened at Effingham called the Lincoln Land amusement place. John and I took Amy & Jenny out there and they had lots of fun. Maybe I can take the boys out there sometime.*

*Love, Grandma Olive*

\* \* \*

Navy orders were usually issued four months before moving from one duty station to another. In the summer of 1979, I started thinking about where I wanted to go and writing home about it. One of the huge disadvantages of my rating was that people in my job were very limited in our choices of duty stations (NavFacs). Most of the bases were either isolated and/or on islands; some of my choices would have been Hawaii, Wales, and an island in the Bahammas. I had had just about all I could take of island life so it was very difficult to decide where to go but I loved the thought of spending a year (or more) in Europe, so Wales was very appealing. Even though I had been told the base would be in a remote part of Wales, I thought that would be my number one choice.

I had to submit three choices on a duty preference form. This form would be sent to an OT "detailer" in Washington, D.C. and he/she would try to place me in one of my three choices. Since I was finishing a year on Adak, I would be in a good position to get my top choice. It gave me something new and interesting to write home about.

## *Letter from Grandma Olive*
*Aug. 31, 1979*

*Dear Kathy,*

Very hot again today. No rain so far. The grass grows faster than the boys can keep it mowed. I guess I will learn to drive the mower while they are in school.

I'm glad you have work to keep you busy. That makes time go faster, I think.

Ralph Thompson & his wife are visiting here. He is my cousin. They are being sent to the Dominican in the Caribbean to organize a Theology Seminary at university level affiliated with Greenville College. They were there many years ago as missionaries.

I think Wales would be a nice place to be. You could get over to Germany ever once in a while. Sunday is our Open House and dedication of the new addition to the church. We are serving cake and punch. I'm to fix the punch. I hope the weather will be nice for it.

Ben Wood races tomorrow night at Louisville, KY. Susie may drive us down. He has been winning 2nd the last 2 weeks...about time for a first.

The boys are having fun with their 3-wheel motorcycle. Troy said it was more fun to ride than a 2-wheel. I think Eric has his car running again too.

Rab is in the hospital again with a heart problem. He is improving a little. I work at Sarah Bush tonight 5-8 at the gift shop. The truckers won the softball tourney at Casey last weekend and go to the National at Stockton, California. They fly out there next Wednesday night and come home Sunday night. Stockton is about 100 minutes east of San Francisco.

*Amy will stay here and go to school. She likes school very well so far. She has Alice Throneburg as a teacher. She has a locker and gets to take a shower after P.E. Quite grown up, eh?*

*The boys say they like school fine too.*

*I must go to work. Take care.*

Love, *G. Olive*

*Pap says hi*

\* \* \*

Eventually, I adjusted to my job on Adak and, in fact, loved it once I was promoted to being a Plotter. After spending several months analyzing sound data, I was promoted to the position of Plotter. In this position, I used the information given to me from the analysts and plotted the positions of the ships and submarines. This information was then provided to the VP squadrons and U.S. submarines to locate Soviet submarines for antisubmarine operations. Plotting made sense to my artistic brain; I loved working over the big plotting table and seeing just how precise I could be in plotting the positions of the ships and submarines. And, finally, there was <u>color</u> in my work world. I used colored pencils to designate the different contacts/targets. That little bit of color made a big difference in my morale at work. The drab gray environment no longer seemed quite as drab.

My supervisor was extremely pleased with how well I performed in that position (he had been less impressed with my abilities as an analyst). I felt elevated to a new level of respect with my superiors and it made a tremendous difference in my attitude about work. Plotting also made me much more aware of what was actually going on in the Pacific Ocean and what my contributions were to the Cold War.

I grew to be very fond of my supervisor, Jim, and his wife, Kathleen. I also became acquainted with some of the Radiomen and Cryptologic Technicians at the NavFac. They were some of my favorite people. I came to realize what all Navy people do; the places you live and work at are as good or bad as the relationships you have with other people.

* * *

One sunny summer day in Adak, I decided I was going to get a suntan. Missing those mornings at the beach in Santa Cruz, I decided to climb a hill in Adak and lay in the sun. I figured even if I pulled up my pant legs and rolled up the sleeves of my shirt, I could at least get a little sun on those parts of my body and my face. I climbed to the top of a hill overlooking the Bering Sea and lay down and closed my eyes. While the temperature might not have felt exactly like summer, it was very pleasant. I had been lying there about 20 minutes when I looked up in the sky and could hardly believe the action going on above me! Two vultures were circling high in the sky above where I was laying. I jumped up and made my way down that hill as fast as I could! I decided the tan wasn't that important.

One of my most frequent leisure activities was shopping at the Navy Exchange - we called it "the Exchange". It was our only store on the island other than the commissary. Not a single week went by without me stopping by there to check out the new merchandise. New shipments arrived every week and usually included items from the mainland in Alaska; clothing, home décor, magazines, Eskimo coats, Eskimo Christmas cards, Eskimo this, Eskimo that. (By the way, looking at those Eskimo items was the closest I ever came to actually seeing an Eskimo.) Everyone loved the Eskimo coats. They were beautiful and so unique compared to any winter coats you could buy in the lower 48 states. I, along with every other Navy person on Adak, had been issued an ugly army-green hooded parka upon arrival to the island. They were warm but not real attractive. Once I saw those Eskimo coats, I knew I had to have one!

Letter-writing was also something I did to pass the time. I enjoyed writing so I wrote lengthy detailed letters about anything and <u>nothing</u>. This is an example of one of the "nothing" letters:

## Letter (excerpt) FROM ME to my mother

*August 31, 1979*

*Dear Mom,*

*How have you been feeling? I have this friend, Kerri, who often asks about you. It always cracks me up because she'll see me in the hallway and she'll say "Hi Kathy, How's your mom doing?" and I always wonder why she specifically asks about <u>you</u>. That's just Kerri. She's kind of hard to figure out. Another continual question is "How have you been doing, Kathy?" The funny thing about this is that she might see me 3 days in a row and, every time, ask the same question. She went up to Marcus one day at work and said "Hi Marcus, How's your mom been?" He said, at the time, he couldn't figure out why she was asking about his mom because he had never even talked to Kerri about his mom! Ha! I guess her conversation is very limited! Ha!*

*Well, I've rambled on long enough. I think I'll go out tonight since it's Friday. It's been a long time since I've had a Friday night off.*

*Later,*

*Love, Kathy*

# Chapter 26

# Whirlwind Romance

In September 1979, my good friend, Marie, flew up to Adak on a P-3 aircraft to see me. I was so excited to have a visitor on Adak! I knew none of my family would be able to visit me there and had assumed Marie wouldn't either. Her visit was like the greatest birthday and Christmas present wrapped in one (even though September wasn't close to my birthday or Christmas).

On Marie's flight to Adak, she experienced the same type of social mingling that I did when I took the hop to Chicago and became acquainted with a few of the guys onboard. When the P-3 landed in Adak, I stood outside on the flight line waiting for the plane to park. The Adak airfield wasn't like a commercial airport. There was no covered walkway for Marie to exit the airplane from and walk into a building out of the weather. The plane would simply taxi over to a certain spot at the terminal and the passengers would de-plane. So I waited patiently for the plane to taxi over to where I was standing.

Once the P-3 came to a stop, I anxiously stood there, peering up at the door of the aircraft, willing it to open. When it finally opened, Marie was one of the first people out of the plane. After she descended the stairway, I ran over to her and gave her a big hug. We were giggling like school girls and so happy to see each other when I heard the man behind her say "Marie, aren't you going to introduce me to your friend?" I hated to be rude but, at this point in time, I really didn't care much about meeting any new guys. Besides, I was deliriously happy to see Marie. However, I allowed myself to be introduced to this man. He then asked Marie if we were going to the club that night. Well, of course we were; there was nothing else to do in Adak in the evening. Marie's friend said he would probably see us there. Marie and I spent the rest of the afternoon catching up.

I had been lucky enough to get a larger barracks room by the time Marie visited me in Adak. A co-worker of mine, Wanda, had left Adak and I moved into her room. Her room was easily twice the size of my first room and it had bunk beds instead of just one twin bed. I was happy to get her room as I had long admired her cleverness at tacking up red floral-designed bed sheets on two of her bedroom walls to resemble wallpaper. Like I said, we were given great freedom to be creative with our barracks rooms on Adak. I loved the bed sheet idea and I liked her room much better than mine. For the few days Marie was in Adak, we spent a lot of time in my room talking, talking, talking.

\* \* \*

On the evening Marie arrived, we went to the enlisted club. The club was basically one very large room with a dance floor in the back of the room. There was nothing fancy at all about that club. I think it might have had one huge disco ball hanging from the ceiling. When we entered the enlisted club, we stood at the front of the club looking for the sailors Marie had met on the P-3. Then, as I looked across the large room, I saw the table the guys were sitting at. Marie's friend, the one I was introduced to, stood up at his table and indicated they had room for us to sit there. As we approached the table, Marie whispered in my ear "I think the one with the mustache is kind of cute." As it turns out, he was the man she had introduced me to earlier in the day. As Marie and I approached the table, the mustachioed man pulled out the chair next to him and motioned for me to sit down. So, I sat beside him.

Marie and I talked with the guys from the P-3 and likely danced with them too. The man I was sitting next to told me a little about himself. He had two little girls and showed me a picture of them. I really had no desire to get involved with anyone that already had children but I was polite and commented on how cute the girls were.

When Marie and I left the club later that evening, I had no idea if I would see or talk to any of those guys again. I would never have predicted on that night that the man with the mustache, George Wolf, would eventually become my husband!

\* \* \*

After Marie returned to California from her short visit to Adak, George stayed in Adak. Marie was only there for about four days but George had a 2-week deployment to complete. I would end up seeing him almost every day of those two weeks.

\* \* \*

**Letter from Susan** (*my sister*)
*September 11, 1979*

*Kathy,*

*Hi! How are you? I suppose by now someone surely wrote and told you that I moved out of mom & dad's. I am renting a real nice little trailer here in town. I like it real well so far but I haven't lived here long enough to have to pay any bills yet. After a month, I might not like it so well.*

*I'm working uptown at the gas station. Joe Oakley is running it now. Joe's a pretty good guy to work for but I'm still trying to get on construction to drive a truck. I could really stand to make twelve dollars an hour but I don't know if I'll get on or not.*

*I guess from what I hear, your life must be a little undecided right now or maybe you've just got too much of a selection of places to go. What about this last guy you wrote about; is it really serious or just another one of those passing things?*

*Well, the big Fall Festival is going to start in two days and I just live a block south behind the doctor's office. So I suppose I'll get right in on all the excitement. Troy is going steady with Amie Ziegler now so he wants to run around at the festival all night Saturday night and then come stay with me. I guess he thinks maybe I'll let him stay out later than Mom & Dad will. I don't know for sure about it yet.*

*Well, as you know, I'm not much on letters so I think I'll close for now. If you want to write back, I'm still getting my mail at mom & dad's box. No more than I get, I couldn't see paying box rent. Take care of yourself and think carefully about the next place you're going so you won't get there and be miserable.*

*Love,*
*Susan*

\* \* \*

George's Navy rating was Aviation Antisubmarine Warfare Operator (AW). He flew on P-3C Orion aircraft from Patrol Squadron Forty (VP-40). He didn't have to fly every day but when he did, he might find himself flying anti-submarine warfare (ASW) missions in the Pacific half way to Hawaii, or flying intelligence-gathering missions off the Kamchatka Peninsula, or perhaps even flying a critically injured sailor or military dependent to Anchorage on a MEDIVAC flight. As an AW, he operated radar systems, electronic countermeasure (ECM) systems, and (primarily) acoustic sensors that used the signal from sonobuoys to detect, localize, and track Soviet submarines.

Our jobs were obviously something we had in common right away; we were both hunters of Soviet submarines. In fact, I was envious of George's job. It seemed far more exciting to hunt submarines from the air than from my dull, windowless environment at the NavFac. I also envied the camaraderie the guys in the VP squadrons had with each other.

George was scheduled to spend two weeks in Adak and we ended up seeing each other almost every day during those two weeks. On days he had to fly, I might not see him or at least not for very long but on other days, I spent most of my time with him. George's strategy for winning my heart involved food. He was clever. On an island like Adak where choices of food and the ability to obtain it are extremely limited at certain times of the day, George couldn't have picked a better way to impress me. I came home from an evening shift one night (it would have been around 11:00 at night) and there was George, in my barracks, with a pizza. It might as well have been a pot of gold. That was the first gesture he made that made me think "What a great guy!"

George stayed in a barracks called "Birchwood" for the duration of his stay in Adak. His barracks were much more modern than mine and much quieter. I loved visiting George at Birchwood because I felt transported to an entirely different world. His room felt more like an apartment than just a room. It was a wonderful escape from the world I had come to know in my barracks where you could hear any and every kind of noise through the walls of the barracks as well as the echo of every footstep in the hallway outside the door to my room.

The greatest thing about visiting George, though, was that he had a way of making me feel like I was the most important person in the world. He made me feel so protected, cared for, and nurtured. I had met lots of wonderful people in the Navy and had gone out with several young sailors but none of them had been like George. He was very loving but also very paternal. As a girl growing up in Toledo, I had always felt so protected by my dad. George made me feel the same way.

After his two weeks in Adak, George flew back to Moffett and immediately volunteered for another 2-week deployment to Adak. So, one month after I met him, we had a second opportunity to get to know each other better. My strongest memory of that time is of him playing his Willie Nelson "Stardust" tape (no CDs back then) which contributed greatly to our romance. By the end of his second visit, our relationship felt more serious and held the possibility of a future together. *Incidentally, on this return trip, George had bribed the manager of the barracks to make sure he got a private room.*

My year in Adak was divided up into two parts: BG – Before George, and AG – After George. The AG part of my year was immensely more satisfying than the BG part. I was a little concerned about the intensity of George's feelings though. It seemed as if he was taking things a bit too fast but it also felt wonderful to be in a committed relationship with someone. By the time I met him, I was really growing weary of the dating scene. I was ready for a long-term commitment to one person.

George was so many things the other men I dated had not been. He was far more interesting than most of the younger guys I had dated (George is 8 years older than me). One of the things that stood out about him right away is that he was selfless; he was always willing to go the extra mile to help me in any way without expecting anything in return. He was giving to the $n$th degree. He also enjoyed art and knew something about it - I loved this about him. I have always been interested in art but had seldom dated any men who knew anything about it. George also loved to read and was very well read; he was very intelligent and seemed to know something about everything. He was also respectful of me in a way that I had seldom found other guys to be and he was extremely affectionate.

While I was very concerned about being involved with a man who already had children, I kept thinking about my dad; how glad I was that he had not let the very same issue prevent him from marrying my mom. Not only had he married mom, who already had two children at the time (my sister and I), but he had always been such a loving and generous stepfather to me and my sister.

When it came down to the wire on deciding where I wanted to get stationed next, I had to take an educated guess on whether or not George and I would stay together. Even though we had only known each other for a few weeks, my relationship with him had been very different than any of the other sailors I had dated in the past. If we were to stay together, I needed to get orders to California (which is what I eventually did).

## Letter from Grandma Virginia
*September 21, 1979*

*Dear Kathy,*

*Hope this finds you well and happy. Grandad is improving every day and has been getting out more. We were up to the bean field 3 times Wednesday.*

*Seems they can't get his blood count up and keep it up. We go every week for a hemoglobin test.*

*But he looks much better and has gained 5 pounds.*

*I have said I wished I had a globe of the world. The other day, Joyce brought us a real nice one so we can follow you around the world.*

*Greg and Travis get off the bus in town and come here of an evening. Billy stays here Monday and Friday so we don't get lonesome.*

*Bill & I went to see Susie Carr's baby last week. She is sure proud of her, Amanda Beth. Has nose like Kenny but fat cheeks like Susie. She was a month later than Susie expected. Susie plans to go back to work November 3.*

*I'm going to go to P.O. and take Bill to Coffee Shop.*

*Take care and write when you have time.*

*Love, Grandma*

The worst years of my Grandad Scott's life were the four years I was in the Navy. In addition to debilitating arthritis and a severe case of glaucoma, Grandad also suffered a few strokes in his last years of life. Grandad was a very soft-spoken, reserved and dignified man. It was hard for the entire family to watch him suffer so much in his final years. On one of my trips home during those years, he cried when he hugged me goodbye. It was obvious he thought that might be the last time he ever saw me.

### Letter from Grandma Olive
*September 26, 1979*

*Dear Kathy,*

*Thanks for the card. It was so nice and came at the right time. I didn't think about Adak being so up to date. Ha ha*

*The weather is so nice here this week. I wish it could continue all winter. I can do without the snow and ice.*

*Jay is cutting beans, doing very well. Some are not ready and some of the corn will be ready soon.*

*We had bible study at Blanche Tippett's this morning. We are studying Romans written by Paul. It is rather hard to understand. I'm glad Joe is there to help translate the meaning to parts of it. I enjoy it very much.*

*I've been working for charity all this week. Monday, I was in charge of the food for the Blood Mobile. Judy & Alice were very good help. They had 86 or 88 donors. Turned 30 away for various reasons. All in all, they thought it was a good turnout. It was by the Red Cross.*

*Today, Amy & I are going down the street collecting for M.S. We have done half of it. I hope to finish today.*

*In the morning, I'm going to the hospital to work in the gift shop for Nellie Massie.*

*John McKinley is poorly. He went to the Carle Hospital for tests. Kenny Evans is there too. His diabetes is out of control.*

*I took Pap to the races last Thursday evening to Henderson, Kentucky. Ben got a 4th. I hope he gets to winning soon. We got home about 1:30 am. It rained down there and all the way home to Olney. Not a drop here at home.*

*What do you need or would you like to have for Christmas? Will you get home?*

*I heard from Brenda yesterday. They are doing o.k. The boys are in football. She says she has a 12-hour day. They are all learning some German.*

*Teresa Owens house is going up fast. It looks very nice. Greg has his started too on the farm. Barb is staying in Aunt Eva's house while she is in the nursing home.*

*Pap is in for supper.*

*Love,*
*Grandma Olive*

## Letter from Scottie (Age 9)
*Postmarked 10/11/79*

*Dear Kathy (with a heart drawn around it)*

*I hope that you liked the letter I sent you. It was raining so I couldn't ride my three-wheeler. Dad is cutting beans and he cut the field behind our house and I ride my three-wheeler out there. I just now made a jump.*

*Greg and Travis were down and they got to ride my three-wheeler. Today, I got your letter you sent me. I just read it and started writing your letter. You said you and Marie had a lot of fun and you done a lot of things. I hope you get to come home in a little bit.*

*You said in your other letter that Adak was so little it seemed like it wouldn't be big enough for a Fall Festival.*

*I thought that it was dumb that a letter has to be 3 inches wide and 5 inches long but they think up some different things.*

*Dad bought Susan a TV set for her trailer. Susan got a dog; its name is Marvin. Susan said it was a boy.*

*The church is having a meeting. It is a lot of fun. We get to go bowling and skating and fun stuff like that.*

*Well, I better go. Write soon.*


*Love ya, Scott*

## *Letter from* **Troy** *(age 11, almost 12)*
*Postmarked 10/11/79*

*Dear Kak,*

How are you? School hasn't changed much. We haven't had any sock hops yet but we should be having one before long.

We had a 4-day weekend this week. I've been helping dad and getting ready for my birthday party. I'm having a weenie roast and hayride. I've been cutting a lot of wood.

It is raining today so we are not farming and I don't have anything to do. At five o'clock, the Boy Scouts are going swimming.

Our church is having a youth group. Scott and I are both in it. We go swimming and rollerskating and bowling. We went bowling about 2 weeks ago.

Last Saturday night, Morgans had a hayride and weenie roast. I went to it and it was pretty fun. There was a car pulled off in a cornfield; everyone jumped off the wagon to soap it. Then it started up and the lights came on and that scared us all.

Yesterday, Greg and Travis brought their motorcycles in and we rode around. We were riding and I drove through some tall weeds and cut two of my fingers in a bunch of places.

Scott flipped his three-wheeler at Max's pond. He didn't get hurt anywhere. Eric was climbing a big pile of sand on Scott's three-wheeler this morning and he didn't get hurt but he got all sandy.

I'm glad you write to me and tell me about your Navy base. I got one of your letters today.

Susan got all moved in to her new trailer and I think she really likes it.

Eric finally got his car fixed up. He has the fastest car at the high school I think. It will go about 140 miles an hour.

Ronnie and Teresa's house is coming along pretty good. I was over there yesterday and they poured concrete in the garage.

Well, my arm is getting tired so I'm going to stop writing now.

Bye
From, Troy

## Letter from Grandma Olive
*October 18, 1979*

Dear Kathy,

We are in a rainy season now it seems. Not so cold. I am under the hair dryer at Gay's and don't have my glasses on so hope you can read this.

John McKinley is worse again and is going back to the Carle Hospital now. You had heard he has cancer of the lung.

I hear you are coming back to California in February. Will you be home for Christmas? Send your Wish List so we will know what you would like to have.

I don't have any ideas what to get anyone this year.

Ben Wood is turned out to pasture for a 3-week's rest. Maybe he will start running again. He will go to Fairmont at East St. Louis next.

Pap hasn't harvested his peanuts yet. The crop won't be too big I don't think.

Home Bureau is at my house tonight. The way it is raining, I don't think many will come. We are serving whip cream and pumpkin pie.

I must sign off.

Love, Grandma Olive

# Chapter 27

# What if the Russians attack?

At 20 years of age, I knew very little of world politics or international relations. Nor did I know much about the Cold War even though I had apparently been dropped smack dab into the middle of it. I had just enough information to be dangerous (in my thought processes). This caused me a slight amount of anxiety when I lay in bed at night pondering my ASW knowledge.

My job at the Naval Facility put me in the position to see evidence of Russian ships and submarines in the Pacific Ocean on a regular basis. My co-workers and I were also aware of American nuclear submarines in the same waters although that wasn't something we could discuss out loud. As if that wasn't enough to stir my imagination, Soviet MIG aircraft also flew in close proximity to Adak. Many nights I lay in bed in my barracks room, hearing the wind howl outside and I envisioned what a nightmare it would be if the Russians took us by surprise and invaded our island. There would be no place to hide. There would be no way to escape.

Growing up in Toledo, the only body of water I was familiar with was the tiny Toledo Reservoir. It was hard to comprehend just how much water surrounded Adak and how treacherous those waters were. However, that was partly what made Adak such a strategic location. At the time, it made sense (to me) that the Russians would benefit by having that piece of land. It would be just a short flight over from their Kamchatka peninsula.

When my imagination went crazy, I envisioned the Russian soldiers leaping out of their boats and charging ashore (like in Europe in World War II). In my mind, they were like the Nazis; they would hunt each and every one of us down like we were animals and then tie us up and do unspeakable things. Actually, I wasn't exactly sure what they would do to us. The focus of my imagination was primarily on the drama of them searching, with their AK-47's, for every man, woman and child on that island. I tried to think of places I could hide even though any efforts at hiding would have been futile.

My grim views of how this scenario would play out were undoubtedly fueled by the fact that we had a rifle cabinet at the NavFac filled with M-16 rifles that were intended to be used if we were ever under attack. We even had drills from time to time to prepare us for that type of situation. The bad thing about Navy drills is that it's easy to adopt an attitude of "this is all just a game, just a waste of time". Not just in the Navy, but in all military services, drills are a routine part of life. My perception of those drills varied. At times, I certainly did feel like it was a waste of time. But, at other times, just the sight of those rifles made me think an attack could actually be a reality.

Dwelling on the possibilities of a Russian attack only exacerbated my increased bouts of homesickness and made me wonder if I'd ever see Toledo again. It was bad enough to think of never seeing my hometown again (or any of my relatives) but the thought of Adak being my final resting place was just about more than I could bear! The fears I had were so emotionally powerful at times. The memories of some of my thought processes during my year in Adak are as vivid as many of my memories of actual people or events.

Chapter 28

# FOOD

*During my year in Adak, I was surprised on two separate occasions
with visits by friends delivering fresh fruit from California.*

**Letter FROM ME to Mom and Dad** *(letter enclosed inside a Halloween Card)*

*Oct. 21, 1979*

## 103

*Dear Mom, Dad, Susan and boys,*

*How's things? In case you're wondering, "103" indicates the days I have left on the rock (Adak). I didn't intend on starting my countdown this soon but I couldn't resist after I received my orders. Lately, I've been getting so bummed out over little things that I've put up with for the past nine months and just can't tolerate much longer. The best example is the food here. There is no place on the island, be it the commissary or junk food machines, that have potato chips with an expiration date later than August. Most are August but quite a few are July!*

*All meat at the commissary is sold frozen. Even though I don't buy meat, I can easily empathize with those who do. On top of being frozen, it costs 2-3 times more than it does in the lower 48 {referring to the lower 48 states}.*

*There is no place on the island, with the exception of the chow hall, that sells anything to eat between the hours of 10:30 pm to 10:30 am. That's really no big deal but I do miss late night get-togethers at "Denny's". Marie and I used to go there faithfully every Friday night, past midnight, for a cup of hot chocolate (for me) and a bowl of clam chowder (for her). Almost always we would end up seeing friends in there and have such a good time just sitting around talking.*

*I won't continue about the food up here (I hate to waste gobs of paper) but I can say this: I hope I never take for granted all the hundreds of neat restaurants in California when I get back there. The first place I'm heading to is 'The Antique' for a good salad, with all kinds of fresh greens in it, and a loaf of their extraordinary bread with melted cheese on the inside. I really miss good bread. All I've had up here is "Wonder Bread" (with the exception of 2 or 3 pieces of homemade bread someone's wife made).*

*Things could be worse; I could be stationed on Shemya. Shemya is a small island (even smaller than Adak) west of Adak near the end of the Aleutian chain. Shemya is totally flat and has only a small Air Force Base there. People can't take their families there. Anyone that goes there goes unaccompanied.*

*Gosh, I sure wish I had the money to back me up on all the different things I want to do when I leave here. Besides coming home, I have a friend in San Diego I want to go see, a friend in L.A. I want to see, in addition to my stopover in Anchorage and possibly Seattle. Oh well, I'm not worried. I may feel like I felt in July; not wanting to do anything but just stay at home and enjoy being back in civilization.*

*I'm looking so forward to getting my car and driving hundreds of miles. I love to drive long distances; that's one of the top five things I miss.*

*Things are going good at work. I'm still working weird hours but I'm in a good position now so I don't mind. There are advantages to working these hours; the main one being that I don't have to get up every morning for work. I never have liked the cruel awakening of an alarm clock first thing in the morning. Also, I think I actually get more time off per week than a day worker does.*

*Well, as you can tell, I've not got any news. The only thing that's been on my mind much are my plans for returning to civilization.*

*Next week, I'm supposed to attend a one-week Leadership & Management Training course at the NavFac. That will be a nice*

*break from my job. The school is from 8-4, Monday thru Friday. It's*
*for E-4's and E-5's to teach us how to be "good leaders". It's pretty*
*much mandatory for all E-4's and E-5's in the Navy providing there's*
*a course given at the Command a person's stationed at.*

*Well, I better hit the rack; it's getting late. Talk to you all in a*
*couple of weeks.*

*Happy Halloween*
*Love, Me*

Reading about the poor variety of food in that letter jogged
memories of mine with regard to homesickness. The subject
of food was a common denominator in the longings I had
about missing home. When I received orders to Adak, I knew
I wouldn't like being cold and wouldn't like being isolated
but the thing I could not have anticipated was just how tiring
the same old food selection would be. Military people around
the world will tell you the subject of food is something most
discussed when it comes to any hardship duty. I longed for the
food from my prior life.

Lasagna and beef stroganoff were specialties mom made
that I often craved. Although, I think the food I reminisced
most about was her chili; in high school, I can remember the
wonderful feeling of walking in the door after a long day at
school and smelling her chili. Mom also made grilled cheese
sandwiches to go with the chili. That was one of my favorite
meals of my teen years. I also missed mom's slushy orange
juice drinks she made for breakfast. She blended orange juice
concentrate with water and ice in her blender and I always
loved how frothy the top of the juice was.

During my teen years, my favorite restaurant mom and dad
took our family to was Tomaso's in Mattoon and my favorite thing

off the menu were the <u>submarine</u> sandwiches (ironic, huh?). SO MANY TIMES, I thought of those submarine sandwiches and yearned for one. They were always served steaming hot and wrapped in aluminum foil like a baked potato. Opening that aluminum foil and inhaling the combination of meat, cheese, and bread was almost as good as eating the sandwich! They were the best submarine sandwiches I've ever tasted.

On Sundays in Adak, I often thought back to Sunday dinners at Grandma Olive's house in Toledo. I can still remember the aroma wafting from her kitchen and dining room. Not only were those Sunday dinners delicious but the entertainment around the dining room was the best! Grandma Olive had a large dining room with a long oval table that accommodated most of the family. All the adults and some of the kids sat around the table and listened to the stories family members told. The Wilson men were the best storytellers! The stories always included heavy doses of humor (and some exaggeration and/or embellishment) and everyone roared with laughter.

When I was a little girl, Grandma Virginia made wonderful breakfasts for my Grandad and my Uncle Charlie. One of my favorite childhood memories was staying all night at her house and waking up to the smell of biscuits and gravy and the sounds of bacon frying, and eggs cooking. Nothing quite compared to Grandma Virginia's breakfasts. However, my favorite food memory at her house was of the hot buttered toast she often made me. As a special treat when I watched TV in her living room, she created a little lounging area comprised of pillows and blankets on the floor. Once I was comfy and cozy, she served hot buttered toast just for me. It was such a simple luxury but so very special because of the love she served along with the toast.

While on Adak, I had lots of dessert fantasies; mom's cherry cheese cake, homemade ice cream at Grandma Virginia's house, and Aunt Joyce's chocolate chip cookies were among the favorites. Not just in the Navy, but all of my life, I've thought back fondly to my Aunt Joyce's chocolate chip cookies. During bouts of homesickness, the memory of those cookies often surfaced. Not only were those cookies scrumptious but I loved spending time with my Aunt Joyce. She was just about my favorite person in the whole world. In the summer when I was a kid, homemade ice cream was one of the most scrumptious treats at Grandma Virginia's house. Grandad was often in charge of keeping the ice cream container moving (that was before automatic ice cream makers) and that helped to make the ice cream memory such a pleasant one. If only I had known how few times in my life I would partake of that treat, I would have eaten twice as much.

Last but not least, Grandma Olive had a grapevine situated along the sidewalk that ran east of her house out into her back yard. As a child, munching on those grapes was one of my favorite summer memories. We kids would eat them right off the grapevine. I don't know that I've ever tasted such good grapes.

\* \* \*

There was nothing more exciting than having a visitor on Adak! I was so fortunate to have a few visitors from Moffett Field during my year on Adak. One of them was the Public Affairs Officer who had talked me into doing that horrible San Jose Mercury article. Maybe he thought he "owed me"; I'm not sure but I was thrilled when he came to Adak! It was SO GOOD to see one of my friends from Moffett Field. That was definitely another highlight of my year on Adak.

## Letter FROM ME to Mom and Dad

*Oct. 27, 1979*

*Dear Mom & Dad,*

*A friend came up from Moffett yesterday along with several other people in an inspecting team. I had no idea he was coming and was really surprised to hear his voice on the phone. He asked me out to lunch and we had such a good time just talking about experiences we've had in the Navy. He was in the Navy 12 years ago. For the past 12 years, he's worked at Moffett as a civilian serving as the Public Affairs Officer. While in the Navy, he once served 2 ½ years in the Antarctic. He said Adak is like a summer resort compared to that place. The operation down in the Antarctic is called "Operation Deep Freeze". Supposedly, the only people that get stationed down there are volunteers. I remember reading about it while I was in California. However, John did not volunteer. He was supposedly sent down there on a temporary assignment but it ended up being 2 ½ years; 2 ½ years without getting to come back to the United States. I think he did get to go to New Zealand though for occasional periods of leave.*

*He's a real optimist. He told me that the Antarctic was really beautiful and that he didn't regret being there at all.*

*He brought me some fresh pears and apples from California. And they're absolutely delicious! I never eat pears except for canned pears. But these are so good & sweet that I've already eaten 3 of them. I just adore people that bring me or send me anything that I can't get up here. I can get fruit at the commissary but it's not near as good as fruit brought up from California.*

*Adak is so beautiful this time of year. It's not near as cloudy but it is colder. And the mountains are slowly being covered with snow. I think it's kind of a perker-upper for me. I love looking at the mountains.*

*I'm trying to limit my phone calls so I'll have a little extra money for Christmas. I'll probably call home the 1st or second week in November.*

       *Love, Kathy*

**Letter from Mom** *(with gift calendar enclosed)*
*November 13, 1979*

*Kathy,*

*This booklet came from Marilyn's store. I thought you might like it, with birthdays marked.*

*Dad & Susan are disking and spreading fertilizer today. I'm cleaning house and doing lots of little odd jobs such as repairing Scott's puppet.*

*Scott has a trumpet and has joined Band at school. He is really excited. Of course, everybody's nerves are shot from him blowing it.*

*Troy thinks he wants to take piano lessons so we are checking into that. I'm going kind of slow in case he changes his mind.*

*Sunday night, they had a quartet at church, The Churchmen, from Oakland. We really enjoyed them, especially Troy. He really likes music so I think maybe he would do okay with a piano.*

      *Love,*
      *Mom*

* * *

Marie had met a sailor at Moffett Field, Dan Adams, and they were serious with each other at this point in time. They would eventually marry in 1981 and have three children.

## Excerpt of a letter from Marie Bourque
*November 14, 1979*

*Dear Kathy,*

*{Dan and I} went car hunting. I was sick and tired of fixing my Volvo so I figured I'd trade it in for something newer. I guess I went to the wrong place because about four hours later, I was driving a new '79 Volvo home. It was all so crazy. The next two weeks were spent applying for loans all over the place. Everyone was convinced I couldn't afford the car. I was beginning to believe it. But, I went over my finances carefully, and found I could. So, I made one last attempt at Bank of America. I talked to the loan agent and he approved my loan. I was so happy.*

*So, we've been going all over the place with this new car. Spending up a storm, too. So, we're slowing down now a little until next week.*

*We've got a new female Chief in Personnel. She's senior to all the other chiefs and I think that freaks them out. She's really quite nice to me and I like her.*

*She's buckled down on us women though as she knows the regs {uniform and hair regulations}. I've been growing my hair and it's been getting pretty long. Well, I was just waiting for someone to say something and she was just the one. So, I've been putting my hair up and it feels really neat to have enough to do it.*

*Good bye for now.*
        *Love, your friend,*
                *Marie*

Yes, as strange as it sounds, Marie was able to drive a car off a dealer's lot without having a loan to pay for it!  Boy, have times changed!

## *Letter from Grandma Ruth Swearingen*
Nov. 19, 1979

*Dear Kathy,*

*Thanks for the card.  We think about you often but just don't get around to writing.*

*Susan tells us that you are in love so I thought I had better write and tell you to be careful. I would love to see you married to a good man you love.  But be sure before you jump into it.*

*Monty went deer hunting this last weekend.  He called this morning and told me he got one.  I'm having the whole family in for Thanksgiving dinner next Sunday.  Wish you could be here.*

*Do you get to come home for Christmas? Next month, you will have another birthday.*

*Susan was out here one day and took a little pup home with her. Never did hear how she got along with it.  I would like to tell her about our dinner but I don't know her phone number.  Love to hear from you.*

*Grandma Ruth*

# Chapter 29

# The Missing Sailor

November 28, 1979

*Dear Mom, Dad, Susan, Eric, Troy & Scottie,*

*So much has happened this week; when it rains, it pours! Tragedy has really hit Adak lately. About a week ago, we had a fire on the island. That seemed to trigger a chain of bad luck. The Child Care center burned to the ground. Luckily no one was in it. The scary thing is that most of our buildings on Adak are very close together. It's practically a miracle no other buildings caught on fire. Our base, houses, and everything is contained on only about ¼ of the island.*

*Next, the roof caved in at the NavFac. The funny thing is that it only caved in on the Operation Officer's office. It was caused by a bad snowstorm we had; winds up to 100 knots. The amazing thing is that it happened during a midwatch and no one even realized it had happened. I was on watch when it happened & the only person that heard it was one of our officers. She went around asking everyone if they heard a loud noise. She got no positive replies from anyone so she just forgot about it. The next day, the ops officer comes to work, unlocks the door to his office, and discovers the roof on the floor! I would have loved to have seen his face!*

One of the worst things that happened was a Filipino lady attempted suicide. She and her husband had a fight and she stabbed herself in the stomach. What's really sad is that she was 3 months pregnant. The hospital put out the word, via television, radio and mouth, that the lady needed "O" positive blood transfusions. Several people poured into Medical that night to donate blood. I have "O" positive but didn't get the word until it was too late.

Last night, another lady tried to kill herself by overdosing on several types of medicine. Her husband is in my section at work. He said he thought that a lot of the problem stemmed from our weird hours at the NavFac. His wife obviously must have other problems but the hours I work DO seem to cause a lot of problems between the married couples. I have no problems understanding why!

On top of it all, I got EMI (extra military instruction) this week for wearing green socks to work instead of black socks. Boy, was I ever humiliated! I always wear 2 pairs of socks to work to keep warm. My green socks were _underneath_ my black socks but my supervisor claims all he remembers seeing is green socks. I told him "Well, you must have been looking up my pant leg to have seen the green socks!" I was so mad! But I came in today for the EMI. All it consisted of was an hour's worth of studying. But the pain was that I got off work last night at 11:00, went in for EMI this morning at 9:00 and had to go to work this afternoon at 2:30 (until 11:00).

Well, there _has_ been a few good things that have happened believe it or not!

First, I received my birthday gift today from you guys. Thank you _so much_! I have been dying to buy this beautiful Eskimo coat at the Exchange for months! I didn't need it in the summer though so I kind of forgot about it. But now that it's cold, I _really_ want it. The money you gave me will allow me to put it on lay-a-way and I ought to have it by the end of December.

*Next, George has been here for the last week and I have been so, so happy. He does the nicest things for me! I love him so much. I've never met anybody so compatible for me! He leaves again on December 10th. I'll be able to see George 2 or 3 times a month from February until July while we're both in California. Then, he goes to Japan until December.*

*He's going to possibly fly up to Anchorage in February to meet me so we can tour Anchorage.*

*I got my written orders in today. This means I can pack-out any time I want to. I may go ahead and have a major pack-out in December and just keep the essential things.*

*Adak has been beautiful lately with all the snow. I've had a reborn love for the island. I try to get outside as much as possible and take long walks in the snow. George and I are going to go tubing if we can get an inner-tube somewhere. This is a fun sport on Adak since it's hilly and mountainous here. People sit in the inner-tubes and just soar down the hills. It looks like so much fun.*

*Well, I'm terribly tired so I think I'll go to bed now. I'll be calling home in a couple of weeks.*

*Love, Kathy*

While I don't remember Adak as being full of drama like the above letter might indicate, I do remember certain strange happenings during my year there. At the top of that strange happenings list was an incident that happened one night when I was working a mid-shift (10pm to 6 am). At the NavFac, I worked in a "section" (group of co-workers) that consisted of a supervisor and 5 or 6 other people. We worked in a large windowless room filled with gray SOSUS equipment, a few computers, a plotting table (for plotting positions of ships and submarines), and usually one or two desks. My work area was about ¼ of the entire size of the room; it consisted of 20 waist-high pieces of SOSUS equipment that produced oceanographic data for me to analyze. It was my job throughout the course of a shift to walk by each of those pieces of equipment to check on the progress of the data every 30 minutes or so. At the end of that long row of equipment was where my computer was located. *(Even though it was 1979, we actually had military e-mail between our base and other bases on the west coast.)*

Just opposite of where I worked was another analyst, Kory, with his own 20 pieces of SOSUS equipment which were also located next to a computer. I liked Kory a lot. He was always so pleasant, even-mannered, and usually pretty positive about life. He had coal black hair cut in the standard short Navy haircut and was very good looking but didn't have the arrogance to go along with his good looks. He was one of the most well-liked guys on Adak. Kory lived in the barracks one building over from mine so I saw him a lot both at work and when we were off work.

On this particular mid-shift, Kory disappeared! I think I was the first to notice so I told my supervisor, Jim, about it. Jim asked everyone in our section if they had any idea where Kory was. No one did. So, Jim asked a male co-worker to assist him in searching for Kory. After thoroughly searching the inside of the NavFac, Jim and our coworker went outside to look around. With blizzard conditions outside, it was not a good night for trying to search for someone. Both men looked in every conceivable location where Kory might be and couldn't find him.

Eventually, Jim and my co-worker returned from their search and told the rest of us they hadn't been able to find Kory. However, Jim thought it prudent to wait a while longer before alerting authorities. The funny thing about military relationships is that you become friends with one another and even if someone has authority over another person, you still don't want to get them in trouble. Jim knew how much trouble Kory might be in if authorities were alerted. And Jim, himself, might have even suffered some consequences of this situation since he was in charge of Kory.

For a short while we speculated on what might have happened to Kory but, eventually, had no choice but to resume our work. One thing was certain; Kory could not have walked back to his barracks; our workplace, the NavFac, was located many miles from the barracks and the weather was far too severe for someone to endure walking that distance. None of us could fathom where our missing sailor might be. It was as if he had just vanished into thin air.

I don't remember how much time passed; maybe 30 minutes (it seemed much longer) when Kory surfaced and appeared back in the room. I was working, analyzing data, when I looked over and saw Kory walk into the room, go straight to his computer, sit down on the stool in front of his computer, and stare into the monitor. I walked over to him, stood at his side, and looked at his face. There was dirt all along one side of his face and he seemed oblivious to it. As I approached him, I said "Kory, where in the world have you been?" and he looked at me, zombie-like, and said "I don't know, Kath" and went back to staring at his computer screen.

A couple days went by and I met Kory in the hallway going to the chow hall. I stopped him and said "Kory, what happened to you at work the other night?" and he confessed he had consumed a significant amount of liquor that day as well as ingested some "speed" but he had no memory of what happened the night he disappeared or any idea of where he went to.

\* \* \*

Those were the times that I wished my Navy life were actually more like the TV show, *McHale's Navy*. While great strides have been made in the military with regard to substance abuse issues, things were way too loose back in the 70's. It was not unusual to walk down the halls of the barracks in Adak and smell marijuana coming from someone's room. That was mild, though, compared to other things that went on. One day, Kory, approached me and asked me if I would do him a favor. I said "What is it?" and he replied "Well, Kath, no one would ever suspect you of doing drugs so I'm wondering if it would be okay if I have a friend of mine mail you some LSD?" I was so flabbergasted at this request (and the knowledge that people actually did things like that) that I hardly knew how to respond. I said "What are you talking about?" and he said "My friend can mail me a sheet of graph paper with LSD on it and I can sell each little square (hit) for $10.00. I'm afraid my mail might be inspected for drugs but no one would ever suspect you of doing anything like that." Needless to say, I declined his request.

### Letter from Scott Wilson (age 9)
*November 29, 1979*

*Dear Kak,*

*How have you been feeling? I hope you are feeling better than me. I'm sick. I got the flu.*

*I am not doing anything so I thought that I'd write you a letter. It's snowing here now. When we woke up, we could not believe it. It was white everywhere.*

*We did not have enough snow to ride the snowmobile. Is it snowing in Adak?*

*Would you send me some pictures of Adak, please. We are studying about Alaska in Science.*

*Well, I wish I had more to say but I don't.*

*Write soon.*
*Love ya,*
*Scott*

## Excerpt from a letter from Marie Bourque
*11 December 1979*

*Dear Kathy,*

*So, how have you been? I've been great! I don't remember if I wrote you about this or not but I caught a hop back to New Hampshire for Thanksgiving. I had a great time. Seeing mom & dad and my brothers and sisters was just what I needed. I've missed them so much -- Mom the most. I miss our talks.*

*Mom was in a real play this year and we all went to see her. She was great!*

*How's your romance with George going? I could hardly believe it when you told me. But I'm very glad for you as he seems like a very nice <u>sensible</u> guy. Isn't love <u>great</u>?!!! I wish I could be near you to hear about it first-hand.*

*Must go for now, Kak. Duty calls. I love you and Merry Christmas.*

*Love, Marie*

# Letter from Roberta (Swearingen) Fritts (my cousin)
Postmarked 11 December 1979

Dear Kathy,

You're not going to believe your eyes. After a year, I finally write. I wished I'd gotten a chance to see you when you were home. I don't get much of a chance to see anyone. Teresa and Christie are busy on their new houses. Teresa's living in her but it's not done inside. They sold their trailer to Kathy and John Glosser so they had to move out.

I start student teaching January 14. I can't wait. I'll do it at Neoga for first grade. Grandma S. was glad to get your card.

Have you met anyone interesting up there? I love to hear you talk about the Navy. I hope I get a chance to see you when you get home.

Christmas is almost here. I can't wait. Kristopher will love it.

Bobby's moving to Charleston to Regency Apts. in January. He's going to Eastern too. He has an undecided major.

Well, I'll end this boring letter. You probably know all of it anyway.

Merry Christmas.
Love, Roberta

For my only Christmas in Alaska, I found and bought some very cute Christmas Cards at the Navy Exchange to send to all my relatives and friends. The illustration on the front of the card was of an Eskimo couple kissing each other. It was in black and white, a pencil and chalk creation by an Alaskan artist. Inside the card, it said:

*Kwi-anotwok Ku sa ma sik elip-nun*
*Ku was win Nu tah mi Ooguwa mi*

This Christmas greeting was written in the Kaweruk Seward Peninsula Dialect, a dialect of the Bering Straits, and translated to: "A Merry Christmas to you and a Glad New Year". Sending those Christmas cards to everyone was one of the highlights of the Adak Christmas season for me.

## Excerpt from a letter from Rita (Brandenburg) Swearingen

*When this letter was written, Rita was married to my uncle, Monty Swearingen. (This letter was included with an Xmas card and gift; a beautiful light blue jewelry box)*

*December 17, 1979*
*Dear Kathy,*

*I bet you thought I'd forget you, didn't you? Well, no such luck. I've just been trying to decide what to get you that would be very practical. Well, if you have already opened this box, you'll see I missed the bulls-eye on the practical end. But the minute I saw this jewel, I thought of you. If I'm not mistaken, it's about the same shade of blue as your eyes. You lucky dog. You always were blessed with the best assets.*

*I'm sorry you can't be here for Christmas but if you can't be here for Xmas, we'll just bring Xmas to you. Silent Night..Holy Night..... Now we got that out of the way, what's new up at the North Pole? Is it cold? Have you had any snow? We haven't. Wouldn't you know, we buy a snowmobile and ride it one year and the next year we can count the tiny little flakes on one hand. Isn't that just my kind of luck?*

*Be sure to come and see us when you get home. I'll be looking forward to seeing you. Bye Bye for now.*

 *Rita*

## Letter from Jeanie Wilson *(my aunt)*
*December 1979*

*Dear Kathy,*

 *I hear we are going to have a wedding in the family. Congratulations. I hope you both will be very happy when the event occurs.*

 *Michelle is going to get contact lenses over Christmas vacation. She hasn't told anyone, so when she goes back to school, she can surprise everyone. Keep them guessing is her idea. Marty found out he will have to wear glasses and is quite excited about it. He doesn't realize the hassle but I imagine it will take him about a week to find out. Then woe is us.*

 *Max purchased a four-apartment house in Greenup this week. I guess we are going to use it as an investment purpose. Not sure of the idea behind it but he is going whole hog on this real estate idea. He is even planning to take Lakeland's real estate course this spring night quarter. He wanted me to take it first but I balked. I told him I teach school, not go there anymore. I imagine I will later if he wants me to and he does go ahead with this idea of his. I want your mom to go with me – J and J Real Estate – how does that sound? (just joking)*

*Take care of yourself – and do have a good birthday.*
*Love, Max, Jeanie and kids*

## *Letter from Bob and Phyllis Swearingen* (my aunt and uncle)
*Postmarked 12/19/79*

*Dear Kathy,*

*We really enjoyed your letter. Congratulations on finding Mr. Right. Is he in the service also? We are real happy for you.*

*Bobby and Roberta are having semester exams this week. Bobby is living there next semester.*

*Diane is living in Greenup now and has an apartment. She has had her divorce a couple of months. Steven & Amy like living there but Diane does miss her house.*

*We are going to Florida after Christmas. Our camper is down there. Roger and family lived in it till they found a house. Bring your fiancé and come out to see us when you get home.*

*Bob, Phyllis & Bobby*

## *Note inside Xmas card from H.A. & Brenda*
*Postmarked 12/20/79*

Kathy,

Thanks so much for the letter, we enjoyed hearing from you. Sorry you won't be home for Christmas. Please write and tell us about <u>George</u>!

Merry Christmas – We miss you.

H.A., Brenda, H.D. Bailey & Jay

## *Letter from Grandma Virginia:*
*December 31, 1979*

*Dear Kathy,*

*I am sure you know that I think of you oftener than I write. Seems I am busy most of the time and don't really get much done.*

*Billy stays here on Mondays & Fridays. Travis and Greg get off here from school. They ride with Eric. Eric is sure good to look after his cousins.*

*I went up to Bradbury to the Xmas program. It was amazing how well Troy did on his piano solo. He seems to have so much feeling & expression for so few lessons. Hope he continues to be interested.*

*They are having a New Year's Eve party at the church tonight. Boys are going. I don't know if your mother was going to go or not. Greg is going with them. Joyce is having Vickie & Malcolm down & Travis is having Ryan Buecher to stay all nite. Joyce said she was going to ask Charlie's. Billy had Travis stay all nite with him. Now he wants "Cott" to stay. He really likes Scotty. Dorothy went back today. She came Xmas day. We were all at Joyce's for supper Wednesday nite. Friday nite, Leland, Charlie's and Dorothy were here for supper. Susie Barz is getting married April 12 and they have bought Grandma Scott's house.*

*Kathy, I hope you have found the right man and you both will be very happy. You will have to tell us more about him. If he is as good to you as George {Joyce's husband} has been to Joyce and you both are as happy as they have been, then George is a good choice. You know I always have and will always want the best for you. In another month, you will be home and Grandad and I will have been married 40 years. The best I could wish for you is 40 years as good as we have had.*

*Grandad is feeling better but he is so thin. Stays between 125# - 130#. Due to the fact he weighed 170# before he got sick, he is thin.*

*We go for a ride about every day but that is about all except to Charlie's, Joyce's and your folks.*

*Better go. Take care and the best to you.*

*Love, Grandma*

Back in California, George was doing everything he could do to help me with my upcoming move. It was really nice to have him to depend on. At this point in time, we had only known each other four months.

**Letter (excerpt) from George**
*12 January 80*

*Hello love,*

*I am so happy — 20 days to go, tomorrow there will be only 19 (TEEN!). It really seems close now! Soon, I'll have you in my arms and soon I'll look into your eyes again. I miss you so much.*

*Norm showed up about 7:30 and we went out for a hamburger. Right now, we're sitting around watching TV waiting for "Saturday Night Live" to come on.*

*I called your insurance agent in Mountain View yesterday. He started your car insurance, full coverage except for medical, effective 11ᵗʰ of January. I'll call him again soon and see how much it is going to cost. That reminds me...I have to call the lady keeping your car today. I hadn't realized that time was so close. I'll let you know what she had to say when I call you tonight...*

*You still need to send me the information about your flight into San Jose; airline, flight #, etc. How long is your layover in Anchorage? When do you leave Adak (times)?*

*You said that you would write me a love letter tonight, didn't you? I hope so. You write GOOD, beautiful, love letters.*

*LATER:*

*It's the next day — only 19 days to go. I couldn't stay up long enough to watch "Saturday Night Live" with Normand. I asked him to leave about 11pm and went to bed. Really slept well, I didn't wake up until about 11am. Normand called after I had eaten breakfast & we went out for coffee. Then we went to the gym and played a couple of games of racquetball. Then we came back to my apartment and are watching TV.*

*I called Linda earlier. She wasn't in so I left a message for her to call me so I can arrange to pick up your car. I'll let you know what she says as soon as I can.*

*I love you very much. I miss you very much. I hope you're doing well these last few days before you leave Adak.*

*I love you and anxiously await your arrival.*

*George*

# Part Six

# Centerville Beach and Ferndale, California

## March 1980-April 1981

The rating badge for my final rank in the Navy.

*Chapter 30*

# Living in a fairytale

G eorge met me at the San Jose airport when I flew in from Alaska. He had picked up my car at Linda's and met me at the airport with it. I think I was almost as happy to see my car as I was to see George! I was so relieved that Linda had turned out to be an honest person and had taken good care of my little Corolla.

My final duty station was a Naval Facility at Centerville Beach, California. When I went through the course there in early 1979, I had no idea I would end up living there one day. That experience helped me become familiar with the area. Moving back there held few surprises. Centerville Beach was located approximately 260 miles north of San Francisco and 100 miles south of the Oregon border. It was situated on 37 acres of rolling pasture land and was five miles away from the nearest town, Ferndale.

Ferndale is a small Victorian style village that could be mistaken for a movie set instead of an actual town. It is so unique that the entire village is considered to be *California Historical Landmark No. 883*. The town is filled with beautifully restored Victorian homes painted in a variety of pastel colors. I was very fortunate to find a small apartment on Main Street in that beautiful little town. Living there was like living in a fairytale. My apartment was located above a candy store and across the street from a bakery. (My poor body has never been the same!) I never tired of seeing the spectacular surroundings in Ferndale.

On my five-mile drive through the country, to and from work, it wasn't unusual for me to come to a complete halt due to cows standing in the middle of the road and not wanting to budge. This always humored me. There were times when I would just sit in my car and laugh. What a contrast that was to being in Adak and seeing bald eagles everywhere.

During my time in northern California, George and I tried to see each other as often as possible. He was still in a deployable squadron which meant he had one final 6-month deployment to Japan. During non-deployment time, he lived in an apartment with his friend, Normand Bissonnette, in Sunnyvale, California. Whenever I got the chance, I drove south to visit him there. It was such a magnificent drive; during that 6-hour drive, I drove through the Redwoods, through scenic mountains, down through the wine valley, over the Golden Gate Bridge, through the hilly city of San Francisco, and on to the city of Sunnyvale where George lived. I loved those trips! I have always enjoyed long-distance driving and was thrilled to be back in a state where I could drive for hours and hours.

Sometimes, George came up to see me in Ferndale. I had my first real apartment (instead of a barracks room) and lived alone. Even though it was nice not having roommates, it could also be lonely so I always welcomed George's visits. Our relationship had become more serious with time and we were completely devoted to each other.

* * *

Once I moved to Ferndale, things were very different with regard to "mail call". For the first time since I joined the Navy, I had a telephone for <u>ME and only me</u>! That completely changed the dynamics of letter-writing and, unfortunately, I didn't get many letters from anyone except George that final one and a half years in California. George's letters compensated for the lack of any other letters though. Seldom did a day pass without receiving at least one letter from him if not more (at least when he was on deployment and he didn't have easy access to a telephone). George's home base for his final deployment was Misawa, Japan, but from there, crews in his squadron also deployed to Thailand, Iran, Diego Garcia, Guam, the Philippines, Okinawa, and South Korea.

**Letter from George** (at Midway Island enroute to Japan)
*2 July 1980*

*Dearest Kathy,*

*Hi baby, well here I am in beautiful Midway. What a dump! The only saving grace so far has been the beach; it's clean and warm. We got in about 3:00 pm, everything was closed, so we went swimming for awhile. I saw a shark and a sea-snake but neither one of them bothered me. I miss you.*

*After swimming, we (the crew) went to chow and the club for a beer. Then I played with the gooney birds for awhile. They're hilarious. The ones on the island are only a couple weeks old and they're really stupid. You can walk right up to them and they just sit there and clack their beaks at you. They're about the size of a goose.*

*I miss you so very much already and know it's going to get worse but we have to be strong and learn to live with it this year. Easy to say but hard to do.*

*I love you,*
*George*

## Letter from George *(from the Philippines)*
*12 July 1980*

*My dear one,*

*I love you. Are you doing well today? I hope so – I'll be glad when I can talk to you again.*

*I'm really beat right now – Norm and I got up early and played nine holes of golf. The course here is right in the middle of the jungle and I lost 5 balls. My game is getting better though. At the end of the game, I figured I must have sweated off at least five pounds in the heat.*

*After we recovered, Norm, I, and 3 other guys off the crew went to the go-kart track and raced go-karts for an hour, then we bowled 2 games. The only thing I won at was the racing – oh well – I'll keep practicing and beat Normand yet!*

*I think about you every minute of the day, baby. I never want to go through this separation business again – from now on, where I go, you go. OK?*

*Well, I'm going to cut this short and try to take a little nap. Please take good care of yourself and keep thinking of me.*

*I LOVE YOU*
*George*

## *Letter (excerpt) from George*
*18 July 1980*

*Hi!*

On one of our flights in the Philippines, we found a small boat that looked like a refugee boat from Vietnam. We called it in and they launched the Ready alert to find it and vector a ship in on it but they couldn't find it again (I'm not surprised, it was so small, you couldn't see it on radar). Anyway, without verification, we didn't qualify for the Humanitarian Service ribbon. WELL, the day after we left the P.I., another VP-40 crew had a flight in the same general area and found our boat again — they vectored a ship in to pick them up and rescued 54 Vietnamese! So, now they're going to give our crew the ribbon ...hooray!

Tonight our officers are going to buy us dinner and drinks to thank us for the flight yesterday — I look forward to it. It's about time the tightwads sprang for something.

I miss you so much it's hard to bear sometimes. I look forward to getting a letter tomorrow and will probably call you on Sunday as a surprise.

I'm going to clean up and go to dinner now.

I love you —
George

When I was in northern California and George was on deployment, one of the ways we communicated with each other was via the autovon line; this was a special telephone line used at work for communicating with other military people on bases throughout the United States and the world.

To use this line, I had to go into an enclosed phone booth at work referred to as the "Bat Booth" (nicknamed from the TV show "Batman"). In the Bat Booth, I could talk privately to George. We were living in two different countries and two different time zones. The autovon line was a godsend at times.

## *Letter from George*
*July 19, 1980*

*Dearest,*

 *Tonight you have a mid-watch. I just got a whole bunch of letters and two packages from you; one of them had your schedule. I never received the letter with the first schedule.*

 *I love you. Thank you, thank you, thank you for the books; they will give me at least 4 months of reading pleasure. I really look forward to starting them. Unfortunately, I left them on my desk – I'll get them tomorrow. Norm and I enjoyed the hot tamales. I also got about 6 letters – hooray!*

 *You write so well – your letters are always the high point of my day (even the one's in which you're depressed).*

*If we don't go flying late tonight, I'll be able to get a frame for your picture. Right now, I've got it on my dresser. Yes, I kiss your picture good-night every night. I wish it were you in the flesh.*

*Tomorrow, your time, you have a mid-watch also – I'll try to call autovon, if I can't get through though, maybe I'll call commercial & send you some money for the phone bill. Well, I'm going to close now and read myself to sleep. I love you.*

*Have a beautiful day.*

G

## Letter from George
*26 July 1980*

*Dear one,*

*How are you today? I hope you're happy.*

*I'm sorry I didn't get to write yesterday evening. About 3 o'clock yesterday afternoon, the hospital called Ops and said that they needed a plane to take a sick girl to a hospital in southern Japan. Well, it just so happened that Norm, my pilots, and I were sitting around getting ready to go back to the barracks – so we volunteered to do it. We were in the air in less than 2 hours and flew down to Yokota, Japan.*

*The girl we took down was in bad shape – she was 18, unwed Air Force, and had had a baby 5 days ago. She had hit her head about six months ago, and started having very bad seizures like epilepsy a couple days ago.*

*Anyway, we got her down there, along with her doctor and nurse, and then found out that the weather in Misawa was too bad to return. So, we stayed there for the night. I got to stay in the BOQ {Bachelor*

*Officer Quarters}. It was really plush — color TV, air-conditioning, etc. — makes my room look like a hovel.*

*So, we flew back this morning…it's just about noon now.*

*The results from the CPO board haven't come out yet here. Chief McKinnan, my chief, said that Navfac Centerville Beach would probably have them a full day before we got them but you're on your 96 {hours off work}. I'm not really very optimistic now. As I said earlier, the zone for selection this year is 16-18 years time in service. Well, there's always the LDO board — and I haven't given up hope yet.*

*I'll try to call you autovon when you get back to work & will call commercial if I make CPO.*

*I love you dear — take care.*

*George*

In the Navy, Chief Petty Officers are selected by a selection board who review all the qualified candidates. They usually select from a "zone" made up of sailors with a certain level of experience and time in service. That particular year, the zone being considered was of people with 16-18 years in the Navy. George only had ten years in at this point in time.

# Chapter 31

# George's Initiation

After weeks of waiting and worrying about whether or not George was selected for Chief Petty Officer, we got the news and it was wonderful news. Despite only having 10 years time in the Navy, he was selected! This was one of the most significant highlights of my first year with George. It was a great way to start our future life together.

The Navy is the only branch of military service where instead of only taking a test to advance to E-7 or higher, sailors go through a 'Selection Board' process in which records of people who scored high enough on the test are reviewed, and then a select few are chosen/'selected to be Chiefs (E-7's).

Initially, a Chief is usually 'frocked' to Chief before being paid for it. In other words, he will be allowed to wear the uniform and possess the rights and benefits of the rank before he actually gets paid for it. This allows all CPO's to be made a Chief on the same day instead of many different days based on pay dates.

The Navy is the only military service that has an initiation ceremony for making E-7. In the past this initiation was very physical and somewhat risqué . In today's world, it has been diluted to a primarily classroom-based process and the old Navy Chief's Initiation has almost disappeared. The idea behind the traditional initiation was to break the candidate down by making him experience many degrading skits and tests, then to elevate him above the rest of the enlisted ranks by making him a Chief.

George had no idea what was in store for him for his initiation; I'm sure he never pictured himself dressed as a Playboy bunny but that's exactly what happened. He was a good sport about all of it even though it had to be embarrassing and humiliating.

### *Letter from George* (sent from Misawa, Japan)
*August 19, 1980*

*Dearest one,*

*How are you this morning? I hope you're feeling fine. I am, today. Yesterday was my initiation; I'll tell you about it in this letter.*

*I love you.*

*Well, let's see. Yesterday morning at 0700, I got up & put on my khakis for the first time, it really felt good (you paid for them by the way). I went over to the CPO barracks with the other 4 guys that made Chief in VP-40 and we sat around and drank coffee with the old chiefs waiting for 0800 to roll-around. We were all acting brave & trying not to show our nervousness.*

*At 0800, we went over to the hangar and attended quarters where the skipper frocked us. After quarters, we went back to the CPO barracks and got into our costumes.*

*My costume was a bright green spandex full-body bathing suit (too small) with a large sequined heart sewn over the crotch to hide my {family jewels}. A bright green dust-mop for a wig with two bright green sequined rabbit ears made out of coat hangers and material, panty-hose (too small), a green ribbon (bow-tie) around my neck, rolled-up socks for breasts, and blue tennis shoes. What a sight! After*

*our flight surgeon (female doctor) put on my make-up, I was beautiful!
Of course, my beard and mustache kind of spoiled the effect.*

*Anyway, after we were made-up, they took us to a building across
base where all the other selectees were waiting. Right away the chiefs
started harassing us. They had us (VP-40) line up in a chorus line
and sing "Anchors Aweigh", "Home on the Range", and "Row Row
Row your Boat" while kicking our legs in the air. The other selectees
from the other commands were terrible but we (VP-40) really got into
it, like the Supremes or something. Right then, I knew we were in
trouble.*

*After they played with us for an hour or so (they had us dancing
with each other, singing "99 Bottles of Beer on the Wall" towards
the end), they packed us up and took us to an old hangar where the
initiation was going to be held.*

*We walked (ran) in and stood in front of the judge (a Master
Chief) and about 110 people, mostly Chiefs, but also 3 Captains,
several commanders, and various other officer ranks; including
3 WAVES {female sailors}. We were told how ugly we were and how
unworthy we were to aspire to being Chiefs, etc.*

*But, they said, since we were selected, they were going to test us to
see how tough we were. First: the physical to see if we were physically
qualified to go through the ordeal. A doctor squirted K-Y jelly into
our hands and told the "women" (the men dressed like I was) to check
their left breast to make sure it hung lower than the right (so – K-Y
jelly all over my left sock). For the men, check to see that their left
testicle hung lower than right (so – you know what..).*

*Second: They must feed us breakfast to make sure we had enough
strength to see through the day. We knelt down in front of troughs
on the floor. Then they came around with ALPO dog food cans and
spooned a bunch of it in front of each of us and told us to eat (without
using our hands, of course. I thought it was only corned-beef hash*

and started eating fast. It wasn't bad but later I found out it really was ALPO! Ugh! But, then they threw a concoction of cold noodles, cherries, pepper, soy sauce, milk, raw liver, raw fish and probably everything else available in front of us to eat. I almost puked looking at it (several guys did). I acted like I ate it trying not to get any on my beard.

After we ate, they split us up into groups. I was going to be in the second group. They drove us back to the first building and actually left us alone long enough to drink a beer, have a few cigarettes, and I even caught a short cat-nap.

About two hours later, they picked us up and took us back to the hangar. They put us in a small room and broke us up into groups of 3 each. I was in Group 7, the next to the last group to go before the judge. While we waited, they had us (1) March in place in two inches of fishy smelling water; (2) Smile, big, for 10 minutes at a time; (3) Play ASW, where one person was a submarine, snaking around in the water and the rest were airplanes snaking around in the water, pinging like sonar; (4) Drink a warm beer in 2 minutes or else; (5) Broke eggs on our heads; (6) Talk while holding an unbroken egg in our mouth; (7) Put ice in our jock-straps (in my case, my panty hose); (8) Tie a string around {my family jewels} and string it out through the top of my outfit so the chiefs could lead me around easier; (9) Take abuse (verbal); (10) etc., etc., etc. It was almost worse than the rest to come.

Well, finally it was my turn. Thanking God that it was almost over, I ran up to the judge with the other two guys in my group and he split us up into individuals so he could "do" us one at a time. They put me in a box with one hole about the size of a beer can with a long, thick, evil smelling cigar, and told me to smoke it down to a stub while I was waiting. (The box was half full of garbage.)

*So, there I sat, listening to them getting the poor guy in front of me, smoking my cigar as fast as I could, listening to the crowd laughing, and trying not to think about what was going to happen to me.*

*The smoke got so thick, I could barely breathe. It was billowing out of the hole in the top of the box (through which people kept cracking eggs and pouring beer, by the way). Someone yelled, "FIRE IN THE HOLE!" I didn't know what he meant until they opened my box and poured in a bucket of ICE water, complete with ice cubes onto my back. At least I saved my cigar. They did that 3 times before they called me to the stand.*

*By then, as you can imagine, my Playboy Bunny outfit was destroyed. I must have really looked pitiful; garbage and eggs and crap all over me, tears running down my face from the smoke. As I walked towards the judge, the crowd screamed "Kiss the Judge, Kiss the Judge!" I was past caring what else they did to me so I started walking around the table towards him. He yelled "If you touch me, it will cost you $100!" I paused for a minute, shrugged my shoulders, said "What the hell" and kissed him on the mouth, hard. The crowd went wild! He (the judge) laughed and said "He's not bad."*

*Anyway, they read my charges & asked me how I plead. I said "Not Guilty". So the judge called the prosecutor to find out if I was telling the truth. He walked up with a goldfish swimming in a cup and told me to eat it if I wasn't guilty. I had been psyching myself up for 3 days to eat goldfish, so – I did. It went down real easy, no sweat. THEN – he handed me a cup of the vilest stuff I've <u>ever</u> seen, smelled, or tasted (truth serum) and told me to drink THAT! Oh boy, did I know I was in trouble now!*

*I took a big sip of it and almost threw-up. I handed it back to him, gagging, and said that I was not going to drink it!*

*So, the judge called out the "Gun Crew" to convince me I should drink it. They had me strip down to my ankles, lay over this sawhorse* type contraption with my butt up in the air, pointed towards the crowd; stuck an egg in the crack of my ass and swatted it with a paddle. Twice. The "crew" pretended like they were loading and firing a big gun.

It was terribly embarrassing.

The judge released me after that, I guess because I was a good sport. They took me back to the barracks; I washed up and put on my khakis for the swearing-in and the CPO creed. They gave us a nice plaque with the creed on it. I'll send it to you soon so it won't warp here in this damp weather.

Well, baby, I've talked to you twice this afternoon on the phone. This is the night you had venison at work. You sounded happy and that makes me happy.

I'm going to sign off now and go to dinner. I love you. I'll write another letter tonight before I go to bed.

I'll love you forever —


George

# Chapter 32

# Getting married

**Letter (excerpt) from George**
*3 September 1980*
*Dearest Honey,*

I ran into an old friend of mine from VP-4 (Hawaii) tonight. He's in VP-50 now; they have a flight staying here for one day. We talked for about 3 hours catching up on all the latest gossip about mutual friends. That's one reason I like the Navy — because you meet old friends all over the world wherever you might be. I haven't seen this guy for about 6 years.

I can't wait until we're married.

When we say our vows, I will concentrate and <u>MEAN</u> them. Speaking of vows, do you want the preacher to say "Love, honor, and obey?" That is up to you; you might want to call him and tell him if you don't. A lot of women wouldn't.

I'm sitting here listening to tapes of music from Adak. It brings back some good memories. I wish you were here to share them with me.

I will write again tomorrow.

I love you,


George


Getting married must have seemed a bit anti-climatic for George after what he went through with his initiation. Making "Chief" in the Navy is a <u>very big deal</u> so we were both very excited about this.

During George's deployment to Japan, he took leave to come back to California to get married. On September 12, 1980, George and I were married in the chapel at Moffett Field. We had only known each other for one year and had been, geographically, in separate places almost the entire year. In some ways, I felt a little like a mail-order bride. So much of our relationship had been phone calls, letters, and short visits. With the luxury of hindsight, it was probably a bit foolhardy to enter into a lifelong relationship that was based on so little time together but George was 100% confident we were doing the right thing and I was about 75% confident.

I had let mom know we were getting married and she mailed me some money so I could buy a wedding dress. (I found a dress in a little boutique for $78.44) She also made airline reservations to come out for the wedding. It was a small miracle that anyone from home could attend the wedding with so little notice. That's my only regret about my wedding. If I could do it over again, I certainly would have planned more in advance and tried to get married at home so all of my family could be there.

* * *

Our wedding day started with George, Mom and I having breakfast at the International House of Pancakes. Then we had several errands to take care of. We had to pick up some flowers from a local florist. I hadn't even considered getting flowers until my mom arrived in California and said "Kathy, don't you think you should have some flowers for your wedding?" To say I was "clueless" would be an understatement. George had to convince me that we needed wedding bands! Would you believe we bought them the very day of our wedding? Yes, that was one of our errands. After taking care of those tasks and showing mom some of the Moffett Field area, we took her out for a late lunch at one of my favorite restaurants "The Antique" (the restaurant I had missed so much when I was living in Adak). We also took mom to a small winery, sampled a few wines, and George bought a bottle of Champagne for our honeymoon. By the time our wedding took place that evening, I think we were all worn out.

I had walked by the Moffett Field Chapel so many times during my year at Moffett Field. It was hard to believe I was actually getting married there. It was a quaint little chapel no larger (and possibly smaller) than the country church I grew up in. Its maximum capacity couldn't have been more than 200 people but that wasn't a problem for us. We had a total of four people in the wedding party and only three guests. Marie was my maid of honor and Ron Druskis, a good friend of George's, was our best man. Marie's husband and Ron's wife also attended the wedding. The only other people in attendance were my mother and, believe it or not, a boy that cleaned the church.

My dress was not a traditional wedding gown but I absolutely loved it. It was cream-colored evening gown with lace on the bodice and a simple A-line floor-length skirt. George wore an inexpensive tan suit he already owned. Marie looked beautiful in a floor-length low-cut pink gown and Ron Druskis wore a suit (also a suit he probably already owned). The ceremony was short, sweet, and to the point. There was no music, no frills, nothing but the services of the Chaplain and, thanks to mom, a few flowers.

After the wedding, George and I, Marie and her husband, Ron and his wife, and my mom all went to a French restaurant in Mountain View and had a wonderful meal. We were seated upstairs in the restaurant in a lovely room with pink and white floral wallpaper and pink tablecloths. I was pleasantly surprised. I had put so little planning into any aspect of the wedding that I had no idea what to expect of our dinner that evening. I don't think we even made a reservation at the restaurant until the last minute. George ordered pepper steak that night and, to this day, he says it's the best pepper steak he's ever had. I remember the soup being very good but don't remember anything else about the food. My main memory of that evening was of the statement I kept repeating to George, "I can't believe we're married!"

\* \* \*

Before leaving on our honeymoon, we took mom to the airport so she could fly down to San Diego to visit our Aunt Mary Matheny before returning to Illinois.

George and I drove up into Oregon to visit Crater Lake for our honeymoon but it was disappointing. There was too much snow on the road to get all the way to the lake and it was also very foggy. Oh well. We weren't really all that concerned with sightseeing anyway. We only had two weeks together and then wouldn't see each other again until George returned from Japan in January. Most of that time was spent at my apartment in Ferndale. Those two weeks went by way too fast and before I knew it, George was once again flying off to be thousands of miles away from me. It was depressing to have our married life begin with him flying back to Japan and myself driving back to Centerville Beach alone. I guess it was a good indoctrination for me being a Navy wife but I didn't much care for it.

At this point in my enlistment, I was simply on auto pilot. I went through the motions to finish out my four years but could only focus on George and I being reunited. I woke up every day happy to be one day closer to April 13th.

### Letter (excerpt) from George *(after returning to Japan)*
*September 27, 1980*

*Good morning my love,*

*It feels funny to sit down and write you a letter again. I still feel as if I could turn around and see you sitting in one of the chairs in my room.*

*I love you. The last two weeks have been the best I've ever had. If we can maintain our love and attitudes at the level we have so far, our marriage will always be a happy one. I'm sure it will.*

*After you left me in San Francisco, I started feeling down which didn't help much in the long flight back here. I flew 5 hours to Honolulu, then waited 2 hours before flying 8 hours to Tokyo. Then, I had to wait 2 hours there until my flight to Misawa; I did get on the early flight out though.*

*I love you and will write more tomorrow.*

*George*

# Chapter 33

# Study, study, study

In the fall of 1980, after we were married, I spent quite a bit of time studying in hopes of advancing in paygrade. Within my four-year-enlistment, the highest rank I could attain was E-5, Petty Officer Second Class. Even though I had no intentions of staying in the Navy, there were a couple of reasons I wanted to advance in rank; not only did it equate to a little extra money for my remaining time in the Navy but I also planned to transfer into the Navy Reserves after my enlistment ended. It wasn't unusual to be reduced one paygrade to go into the Reserves so I felt like I needed to end my enlistment with the highest paygrade possible.

In order to make E-5, I had to study a manual about my rating, Ocean Systems Technician. Because this information was classified, I could not study in my apartment. So, on my days off, it was not unusual for me to spend time at the NavFac studying. The subjects included oceanography, physics of sound, anti-submarine warfare, etc. There are several steps in advancing in the Navy. Not only was I required to take a written test, but I had to be subjected to an oral board with at least six of my superiors asking me questions of their choosing. No matter how well I performed, there were no guarantees of advancement. I just had to do my best and hope everything would fall into place.

## *Letter from George* *(from Japan)*
*October 5, 1980*

*Dearest love,*

*I just received a letter from you, the 43rd letter you've sent me since I left in September.*

*I love you.*

*I also received the jelly beans you sent me, the ones that cost $1.00 to buy and $1.32 to send to me.*

*I adore you.*

*I am reading this letter to you on the phone now –*

*Take Care – love me*

*ILY*

*George*

## *Letter from George* *(from Japan)*
*October 13, 1980*

*Dearest my true-love,*

*How are you this morning, my darling? I hope you're feeling well and happy. I hope you've started getting some mail also!*

*It's about 10pm on Monday, the 13th. Another Chief is leaving tomorrow for the states and I'm going to give this to him to mail at Moffett. The post office here wasn't open today because of Columbus Day so there are at least 5 letters sitting inside it that I wish I had kept now and sent with this guy.*

*I love you very much.*

*The letter my mom sent you was a very good letter. The advice she gave us is very good. I hope I'll still make your heart beat faster on our 30th wedding anniversary!*

Take care of yourself.  I said a prayer last night & will again tonight and tomorrow to help you pass your tests.  If you don't, don't feel bad. Please.  I've failed exams in the Navy before... all you can do is regroup, study, and try again.

I love you.  I miss you.  I need you.  I want you.

George, your husband

## Letter from George
*October 15, 1980*

Hello Baby,

It's about midnight; I went to sleep early (about 7pm)...you called a few minutes ago to tell me the good news.  You passed your test. HOORAY!!  I'm so proud of you, I knew you could do it if you tried and you've really been studying hard lately for it.

I love you.

I'm proud of you.

I'm not going to write a long letter tonight as I want to go back to sleep.  I don't know why but I'm really tired tonight.

I hope you've started getting mail again, baby; I'll keep the letters coming...at least one a day.

Be happy today and I'll take time out to write a nice LONG, LOVING letter tomorrow.

I love you,

George

> Sometimes when George had an exciting flight, he would write about the event in a letter. The P-3's ASW missions required flying only 100 feet above the surface of the ocean. While many of his flights were exciting, they could also be quite harrowing.

## *Letter from George* (*from Misawa, Japan*)

*November 2, 1980*

*Hello my love,*

*As you know, while we were talking last night, I got launched. We went flying to the Sea of Okhotsk, Russian waters. We monitored buoys/grams for six hours before finding him {a submarine}, then only got to stay with him for 1 ½ hours before we ran out of gas and had to go home. I was so tired when I got home, I was afraid I'd miss your call. As you know, I was a little incoherent when I talked to you the first time.*

*After I talked to you at 8pm, I found a note on my door that I could go to Osan {Korea} tomorrow if I wanted to. I'm going to go; I'll buy us a blanket/quilt and some sweaters for you. I only have $100 to spend but I'm sure I can get us some really nice things with that amount.*

*I know I'll miss about 5 hours of being able to talk to you by going to Korea, and I hate it, but I've been trying to get there for 3 weeks and want to get the gifts/stuff in the mail so you'll have it for Christmas.*

*I love you. I miss you.*

*Well, by the time you get this letter, the presidential election will be over. I hope Carter wins. I'm afraid if Reagan wins, we'll be in another war within a year. I have too much to live for (you) to get involved in another war. During Vietnam, I was a single guy and didn't really worry about it. Now I do. I love you.*

*It's about 12:30 pm now -- you might call before leaving work. I'm going to close and get some sleep before going to Osan. I'm still tired from the flight yesterday/today.*

*I love you and dream of you constantly.*

> *Forever,*
>     *George*

### Letter from Scott Wilson *(age 10)*
*November 6, 1980*
*Dear Kathy,*


*I am sick today so I thought I would write you a letter. I haven't wrote anybody in a long time (even you). How is it having your name be "Kathy Wolf"? Or being married?*

*I'm sorry we haven't got our pictures yet from school. When we do, you will be the first one to get one.*

*Our report cards come out Friday (I hope I get good grades). The trees are beautiful with their color. Well, I don't have much to say and I got to watch cartoons.*

*Love, Scott*


This was the final letter I received during my Navy years from any of my brothers. It seems fitting that it was from my "baby" brother, Scott (whom I always called "Scottie"). Leaving him behind when I joined the Navy was the hardest part of leaving Toledo. I was 11 years old when he was born and he was the "light of my life" during my final years at home.

# Chapter 34

# Earthquake!!

I guess it really shouldn't surprise anyone living in California if they end up in an earthquake but it did me! At 2:27 am, on November 12, 1980, I awoke to my bedroom shaking. I could feel my bed moving and hear the pictures on my bedroom wall rattling. I was so shocked at what was happening, my only thought was to phone home to let my parents know that I might not survive the earthquake. I guess it was due to the excitement of the moment that I dialed a wrong number. And even though the man who answered was not my dad, I had a hard time accepting that until he finally said "Honey, I'm not your dad, you better hang up the phone and try again." So, I did and that time, my mom answered. I told her what was happening, she asked me a couple of questions, and then she said "You need to get out of your building". So, I got dressed real quick and ran downstairs and was surprised at what I saw. Even though it was the middle of the night, there were men and women on Main St. walking up and down the sidewalks looking at the damage to storefronts. The earthquake had measured 7.1 on the richter scale and lasted 30-40 seconds.

Broken windows and chimneys accounted for the primary damage but a few people reported homes off their foundations and gas lines severed. The worst damage occurred when an overpass collapsed onto Highway 101; seconds later, a Volkswagen bug and flatbed truck plummeted 30 feet off the overpass. The driver of the Volkswagen sustained serious injuries and his two 9-year-old twin sons were critically injured.

We had many aftershocks after that earthquake and it seemed weeks before things were back to normal. Sometimes at night, when I would lay down in my bed, I wasn't sure if my bed was moving or if it were my imagination.

*Excerpt from Letter from George* (with article from newspaper in Japan)
*November 10, 1980*

*Dearest love,*

*I'm so glad you weren't hurt in the earthquake! I don't know what I would have done if I hadn't heard from you. As you can see, the paper here made a pretty big deal of it — I'll bet you were terrified! But now, you can say "I lived through the earthquake of 80."*

*Everyone here started talking about quakes they've been through as soon as word got out. I think I'm the only one in the squadron with any loved ones affected though.*

*I love you.*

*I stayed home sick today. This cold has got to go!! I'm thinking about just staying home for 2-3 days and sleeping all day. I don't know. I don't get sick too often, but when I do, I have a hard time getting rid of it.*

*I'm going to close this letter now. You should be calling again soon. I love you.*

*Forever and totally yours,*
*George*

## Letter from George
*December 13, 1980*

*Dearest love,*

*Happy Birthday to you, Happy Birthday my dear one…Happy Birthday to YOU! Happy 22nd birthday, baby doll. I wish I were there to give you an appropriate gift (me!). I love you and hope to make your 23rd year the best one in your life yet! I love you.*

*As you know, I've been running NCCM Johnson around the last two days. I really like him but I'm kind of glad he's gone now. I was getting so tired (physically) of running around for him and the Admiral. These have been, without a doubt, the two most nerve-racking and tiring days I've had this deployment.*

*I'm glad you used to work for him. It was a real ice-breaker when I was able to use your name. He was really surprised and delighted for you and me. He was interested in your career and what you had been doing for the last couple of years. He said you were one of the hardest working and dedicated people he'd ever had work for him. He really got a kick out of the story about how you went on a diet and jogging stint when he mentioned you were "gaining weight". He laughed and said he remembered the day he said it and also remembered that you started losing weight.*

*Did you know that he has been in the Navy, Marines, and the Army? The guy is pretty amazing. If I were around him for a time, I could just see myself being affected by his presence and trying to be like him.*

*He remembers you fondly and said to make sure you stay in the Reserves and I think he'll enjoy seeing you when we return to Moffett.*

*He seemed pretty impressed with the squadron and (hopefully) with the job I've been doing. At least, the last words he said to me were "I'm really impressed with your troops". So, maybe I've done good.*

*I love you. Only 24 DTG! {days to go}*

*George*

# Chapter 35

# The Worst Moment of My Life

Throughout December of 1980 and January 1981, George and I had been counting down the days until his return from Japan. We were looking so forward to being back together again. We had been married for four months but had only been able to spend our two-week honeymoon together.

On that final week of waiting to be reunited, and being reunited, we had a double shock. First of all, my granddad, Bill Scott, died on January 4th. It became apparent that he would not live beyond that week so I flew home in order to see him before he died. Granddad had suffered the entire time I was in the Navy with poor health. His funeral and burial was on January 6th. The very next day, my dad took me to the airport in St. Louis so I could fly back to California in time to meet George on the 8th.

On January 8th, 1981, George finally arrived back in California. I drove to the hangar at Moffett Field where George's squadron would be arriving. The scene in the hangar was the classic sailors-returning-home scene; lots of women and children standing around anxiously awaiting the arrival of their beloved sailors. I stood alone, dressed in a brown and beige summer dress waiting for my new husband to land and enter the hangar.

When the plane landed, the guys slowly trickled into the hangar where the families were. There wasn't a grand entrance of many sailors arriving at the same time. At least, that's my memory of it. I watched each and every sailor enter the hangar, anxious to locate George. Finally, when we spotted each other, he ran over to me and hugged me and hugged me and hugged me. In that moment, I became oblivious to anyone around me or to anything else going on in the hangar. It was just he and I. We soon departed the hangar and drove to a nearby hotel where we would spend the night before heading up to my apartment in northern California. We were so glad his deployment had ended and were really looking forward to spending more time together as a married couple.

We had only been in the hotel room for a few hours when, around 1:00 in the morning (California time), the phone rang. I instantly had a bad feeling. I knew that my mom was the only person on the planet who knew where we were staying that night. George answered the phone. I heard him say a few words, he hung up the phone, and then he wrapped his arms around me and gave me the worst news of my life; my dad had been killed in a car wreck.

At first, I clung to the slim possibility that the phone call was some kind of horrible mistake. I phoned my Aunt Joyce in St. Louis and asked her if she was aware of any bad news from home. After she confirmed the tragic news, I hung up, went into the bathroom, and was immediately sick. And, then, it was as if the planet quit rotating on its axis. I can remember feeling that way; that not just my life but the entire world had come to a screeching halt. In the darkness of that hotel room, it seemed like everything just stopped.

Almost instantly, I realized what day this was; it was my mother's 40<sup>th</sup> birthday. It all seemed so surreal. She had just lost her own father 5 days earlier. How could this be happening to her? How could this be happening to our family? I had just been home for my Granddad's funeral and my dad had only taken me back to the airport less than 48 hours earlier!

I struggled to make sense of all this. Suddenly, in the darkness of that hotel room though, I realized I had been given a "gift" at the airport. My dad and a family friend, Lee Pennington, had driven me to the St. Louis airport. They had walked with me into the airport and stood talking for awhile. When it came time for them to leave the airport, my dad had looked at me and said "Are you sure you want us to leave now?" and, for some reason, I said "No..., let's go have a drink somewhere". This was really unlike me and never before, or since, have I done anything like that. So, there we were; Dad, Lee and I in the St. Louis airport, spending another few minutes together. Then, it was time for me to go; my dad gave me another big bear hug and we unwittingly said our final good-byes to each other.

I've always considered that extra time with Dad a gift from God.

* * *

I was almost four years old when my mom married my dad. I don't ever remember a time when my sister and I didn't call him "dad"; he was always "dad" to me in every possible way. He was the most loving stepfather/father a girl could have and I will always be so thankful for his love, his guidance, and his support throughout my childhood. He enjoyed/endured all the joys and the crises of my childhood and teenage years along with my mother.

*Jay Wilson*

## Jay Wilson Killed In Truck Crash

Jay F. Wilson, 41, of Toledo was killed Friday morning when the 4-wheel drive pickup truck he was driving on an icy road (Toledo-Jewett Road) one and one-half miles south of Toledo, went into a ditch, hit a light pole and overturned. The cab caved in when it landed upside down.

He was apparently killed instantly, according to Cumberland County Coroner Mike Barkley who declared him dead at the scene at 1:45 a.m. January 9.

Obituary is in this edition on another page.

Used with permission of Toledo Democrat

Dad was like a big kid in many ways; he loved buying new "toys", new gadgets, and things that were "cutting edge". I think we were one of the first families in Toledo to have a color TV, one of the first families to have an electric dishwasher, and he also had a thing for the latest in wrist watches. Dad loved cars and surprised us from time to time by showing up at home with unique vehicles. He came home one day with a metallic pink Thunderbird that had "suicide" doors (the back doors of the car opened backwards). I thought that was the coolest thing I had ever seen (because it was)!

Some of my favorite memories are of the toys Dad bought for us kids. The most magical toy of my childhood was a little replica Model-T car that Dad surprised us with. We had an asphalt driveway in front of our house and we had so much fun driving that little car around on the driveway. Dad bought us motorcycles, three-wheelers, cars when we turned 16, etc. He was so kind-hearted and never treated me or my sister any differently than he treated his own three sons. If you asked him how many kids he had, he would always say "two girls and three boys". Although our family lost him way too soon, I'm so thankful for the years that I had him in my life.

* * *

After George and I returned to California from Dad's funeral, I had three months remaining in the Navy. During that time, Ronald Reagan was elected President of the United States and he was nearly assassinated by John Hinkley, Jr. but that meant very little to me compared to losing my father.

# Chapter 36

# Journey with an Amnesiac Sailor

The final adventure of my Navy years was the somewhat unusual duty of driving a medical patient from my base, Centerville Beach, to the Naval Regional Medical Center at Oakland, California. At smaller Navy bases, people are often tasked with extra duties that have little to do with their actual job. Having no professional connection to any of the medical personnel on our base, I was probably chosen for the driving duty simply because I was available and agreed to do it. Since I was only three weeks away from being discharged from the Navy, I had been taken off shift work and therefore had much more flexibility during the day.

A Hospital Corpsman, Jacob, accompanied me and the medical patient, Robert, on our six-hour journey to Oakland. The Centerville Beach medical facility offered only minimal services so it had been determined that Robert would undergo further evaluation at the larger medical facility in Oakland. The military was much like the civilian world; small medical facilities often sent patients to larger hospitals for any medical issues requiring the advice of specialists.

On March 25th, 1981, we set off on this unique trip. I was in the driver's seat, of course, and Jacob and Robert were together in the back seat. This arrangement made me feel like Jacob might be a mild threat which increased the dramatic flavor of the journey. I've always been fascinated by the many things that can go wrong with the human brain so I had to stifle my excitement over this rare opportunity to spend 6 hours with an alleged amnesiac! Most of the Navy people associated with Robert's case were skeptical regarding the validity of the amnesia (myself included). This made it all the more fun to spend time with this guy, converse with him, and try to figure out if the amnesia was legitimate. I had never known a person claiming to have amnesia but had been fascinated with every case I learned about via TV or in newspapers or magazines. Having no formal education in matters of the brain, I doubt that I even realized there were different types of amnesia at that time in my life. On the other hand, I felt I had developed pretty good instincts when it came to liars.

We took off early in the morning, knowing we would have to stop for lunch on our way to the hospital. I've always loved road trips so I viewed this as another great opportunity for a road trip even though the company I was keeping was definitely a bit on the weird side. The corpsman and I had no great rapport but I naturally felt aligned with him in this unusual situation. He and I attempted to engage in small talk with Robert but Robert's answers left us frustrated. Heading south on Highway 101, we drove through the Redwoods and I exclaimed "Look at the trees! Aren't they beautiful?" and Robert answered "What's a tree?" Later, when I spotted a vineyard along the highway, I said "I'm fascinated by vineyards" and glanced over at it. Robert said "What's a vineyard?" Jacob and I grew weary in a very short time with Robert's standard reply. His answers seemed too calculated. There was so little deviation in them.

It came as a great relief when we had driven far enough to declare it "lunch time". Jacob and I decided to stop at a

McDonald's and go inside. While ordering our food, I asked Robert if he wanted french fries, and...surprise.., he said "What are french fries?" That's when I nearly came unglued. For some reason, his other "What are..." questions hadn't bothered me nearly as much as the one about french fries. That question was the one that sealed the deal on my conclusion that his "amnesia" was a complete charade. The guy was lying. I felt as sure of this as I was of the sun coming up every morning. I just couldn't prove it.

By the time we reached the hospital in Oakland, I was more than ready to end my brief association with Robert. Whether or not he had amnesia was almost moot. I was just tired of dealing with him. After Robert was checked in at the hospital, Jacob and I bid him farewell and headed back to Centerville Beach. The trip was rather dull. Jacob and I discussed the issue of Robert's amnesia ad nauseam. Both of us were sure Robert was trying to manipulate everyone, including us, in an effort to seek attention and possibly get out of the Navy. People did crazy things to get out of their military service contracts (and undoubtedly still do). For sailors "lucky" enough to get a medical discharge, not only is their enlistment shortened but they often end up with disability pay for the rest of their lives (as well as other benefits for disabled veterans).

From what little I knew about amnesia, victims of that rare diagnosis lose parts of their memory regarding personal history but not an entire vocabulary. I just couldn't get past Robert's supposed inability to understand the words "french fries".

Because medical diagnoses are confidential and the Oakland hospital was located so far from Centerville Beach, I never did find out what Robert's doctors concluded regarding his amnesia. I would bet money, though, that they saw through him right away.

In my four years in the Navy, I had come across a wide variety of characters but Robert has the distinction of being the only sailor I ever knew who had claimed and/or feigned amnesia.

# Chapter 37

# Easy Street

My four years in the Navy ended on April 13, 1981. Driving off the Centerville Beach base and away from my active duty obligations felt like pure freedom. For all the good things I had experienced in the Navy, the one thing many military people feel is a lack of freedom. When you're in the military, you have to be available to your superiors 24/7. There is no pay for working overtime and it's not unusual to work overtime on a weekly basis.

It was hard to believe that my enlistment was finished. That period of time, in so many ways, had seemed like a lifetime. My whole world had changed. And my family's life in Toledo had changed. I've often wondered what I would have thought if I had had the ability to look in a crystal ball four years earlier and see the future. I'm pretty sure I would have thought the crystal ball was defective. It would have seemed too preposterous that, in only four years, all the events that happened to me and my family could actually have happened.

On the day I was discharged from the Navy, I was excited to be starting a whole new chapter of my life. I was finally going to be able to live with my husband of seven months and would be back in the Moffett Field area which I had grown so fond of. I had applied for a position with the Defense Advanced Research Projects Agency (DARPA) at Moffett Field and had been hired. I was hired because of my knowledge of antisubmarine warfare which was pretty amazing since I assumed I would never work in that field again.  George and I were very fortunate to both be working on base.  This was a godsend since we only had one car.

George and I found a little one-bedroom apartment located just a few miles from Moffett Field, in Mountain View, California.  That little apartment consisted of a small kitchen, small living room, one bedroom, and one bathroom but it seemed like the most wonderful place in the world to me!  Our apartment was only a ten-minute drive from where we both worked at Moffett Field and it was a short drive from all my favorite places in that area.  We hoped it was a good omen that our first street address of our new life together was 335 <u>Easy Street!</u>  I can remember Grandma Olive getting such a kick out of that; the first time I saw her after moving there, she exclaimed "Here, I've been trying my whole life to make it to 'Easy Street' and you're already there!"

# EPILOGUE

Nothing remains the same. Many of the elements of my story of 1977-1981 have dramatically changed or no longer exist.

The Recruit Training Facility in Orlando no longer exists. In today's Navy, all male and female recruits go through Basic Training at the Navy base in Great Lakes, Illinois.

After weathering three earthquakes in 1992, NAVFAC Centerville Beach was decommissioned in September 1993. The property is now being managed by the Bureau of Land Management and is being converted into a scenic property for public use. The current property will offer nature trails and access to beaches and coastal streams. All the buildings of the former Naval Facility have been destroyed.

The Naval Air Station Moffett Field closed in 1994 and was turned over to the NASA Ames Research Center.

On March 31, 1997, The Adak Naval Air Facility closed. It became one of the casualties of the Base Realignment and Closure Commission.

Of all the bases I was stationed at during my enlistment in the Navy, the Norfolk base is the only base that still functions as a Navy base but there is no longer an OT "A" school. My Navy rating, Ocean Systems Technician, no longer exists. In October, 1995, the OT rating was merged with the Sonar Technician-Surface (STG) rating. All Ocean Systems Technicians became Sonar Technicians.

A couple years after I finished boot camp, I was neither sad nor surprised to hear my first Company Commander, Petty Officer Franklin, had been kicked out of the Navy for being gay. The details surrounding her expulsion from the military were a bit murky but it was thought that she had been caught red-handed in a love affair with another woman (which is the other way, besides admitting homosexuality, to get kicked out of the Navy for being gay).

Master Chief Courtland "Corky" Johnson, who had made such an impression on me my first year in the Navy, passed away on May 23, 2003. Thanks to the internet, I discovered that he not only served in 3 branches of the military but is likely the only man in America who served faithfully in <u>five branches</u> of the United States Military; he served in the Marine Corps, the Navy, the Army, the Army Air Corps (no Air Force back then), and the Merchant Marines. *(The Merchant Marines is considered to be an auxiliary of the U.S. Navy during wartime.)*

My friend, Marie, never left California. She resides there with her second husband, Brad. Marie and I have seen each other several times since my enlistment ended and she will always be a friend and blood sister of mine.

Bob Zafran lives in Oregon and is still very involved with his old "shipmates". He has been integral in arranging VP reunions for many years. Bob is one of the most faithful friends anyone could have.

**One of the greatest joys of writing this book was reconnecting with Navy friends whom I had been out of touch with since my Navy years:**

Simply by using Google, I found my boot camp friend, Anne. She still lives in California and has become a Professor of Sociology. Anne and I ended up communicating back and forth for a couple of weeks and I discovered, among other things, that she and I we were both married only one day apart from each other back in 1980!

Through Facebook, I reconnected with my friend/roommate, Joslyn, from Centerville Beach. On a whim, as I was writing Chapter 21 about Joslyn and her grandmother, I typed her maiden name into the Facebook search box and voilà, there she was! I could hardly believe my eyes. The next day, we chatted on Facebook, she gave me her phone number and we talked for about two hours on the phone that evening! It has been wonderful reminiscing with her and I'm grateful for her assistance with Chapter 21. Joslyn resides in Florida.

Facebook also made it possible for me to reconnect with my friend, Rosemary, whom I knew when I was stationed at Centerville Beach. It's been so nice getting reacquainted with her. She now lives in upstate New York.

And just when I thought I couldn't possibly reconnect with anyone else mentioned in this book, Bob Zafran put me in touch with John Shackleton on the final day of finishing the book! John still lives in the bay area south of San Francisco.

# Acknowledgements

I owe so much to my devoted and wonderful husband, George, for helping me to make this dream of writing a book a reality. George has given me nothing but unconditional love, encouragement, support, and guidance throughout every step of this incredible project and he's spent many, many hours helping me with numerous details of writing and publishing this book. He's the best.

I'm also very grateful to my son, Adam, and son-in-law, James Fiscus, who helped to edit several parts of the book. They are both talented writers and made great suggestions for improving my book. My son also contributed in numerous other ways and was always so willing to help in any way. Thanks to my daughter, Stacy, for simply calling me to talk when I was at my computer typing away and desperately needing a break. Those calls were morale boosters when I was sitting alone at my computer wondering if I would ever get the book finished.

My mother, Judy Wilson, also helped in myriad ways in the early weeks when I was trying to pull all this material together. She gave me the clarification I needed on many names, facts, and situations regarding details in the letters from Toledo. She read an early rough draft and gave me her seal of approval. That meant a lot.

My friend, Marie, also read an early draft of the book which helped to give me confidence in finishing the project. Her four-hour phone call to me at the beginning of the project was simply wonderful and filled me with enthusiasm for writing the book.

I'm also grateful to the people I contacted whose permission I felt I needed to print their letters and/or write about them. You know who you are. Thanks so much.

Thanks to my friends and family members who have been encouraging throughout this process. I am especially thankful to my good friend, Jo Chiparo, who has been one of my most supportive "cheerleaders" since the first week of this project. I am constantly inspired by her.

# About the author

After Kathy's enlistment ended in 1981, she spent the next ten years living with her husband and children in the Azores, Texas, Iceland and Indiana. After her husband's retirement from the Navy in 1991, Kathy and her family settled in Bloomfield, Indiana. Kathy worked in the Bloomfield Public Library for 14 years before going back to school in 2007 to obtain an Associate's Degree in Criminal Justice. She will be transferring to Indiana University in the fall to pursue her Bachelor's Degree in Criminal Justice. She enjoys reading, travelling, bonding with foreign students, and spending time with family.

Made in the USA
Lexington, KY
20 August 2010